A Matter of...
FACT

A Look at More Evidence for Christianity

Kyle Butt, M.A.

APOLOGETICS PRESS

Apologetics Press, Inc.

230 Landmark Drive

Montgomery, Alabama 36117-2752

© Copyright 2002

ISBN-10: 0-932859-47-X

ISBN-13: 978-0-932859-47-1

Library of Congress Cataloging-in-Publication

Butt, Kyle, 1976 -

A Matter of Fact: A Look at More Evidence for Christianity / Kyle Butt

ISBN-10: 0-932859-47-X
ISBN-13: 978-0-932859-47-1

1. Apologetics and polemics. 2. Science and religion. 3. Creation. I. Title

213—dc21   2002105358

DEDICATION

To my dad, Stan Butt Sr.—truly, the glory of children is their father (Proverbs 17:6).

TABLE OF CONTENTS

FOREWORD

A single bead of sweat rolled down his face as he stared at the four wires—yellow, blue, white, green. For the past two years, Joe had been training for this type of mission, but as he watched enemy tanks drawing closer to the bridge, all those instructions were jumbled in his mind. He had about two minutes and thirty seconds until they reached the bridge—plenty of time to connect a few wires; but remembering which wire to connect to which metal post proved to be much more difficult. Joe did remember one fact; the white wire always plugs into the farthest left terminal. He confidently steadied his shaking hand and twisted the wire around the metal clip. The tanks were drawing closer—and he still had three wires to connect.

Joe knew that if he didn't destroy the bridge in time, his unit would be crushed by the deadly force of the enemy attack. As much as he needed to concentrate, he couldn't keep his mind from drifting to thoughts of his girlfriend. They had dated for three years in high school, and for the past two years had been talking about getting married when his time in the military was finished. He wondered if he would ever see her again. Would she marry someone else? Would she live the rest of her life without marrying?

The rumbling of the tanks and verbal shouts from the enemy interrupted his thoughts. He had wasted about a minute of his precious time, and now he estimated his remaining time at 50 seconds. Feeling fairly confident in his next choice, he remembered that the green wire usually hooks in directly beside the white one on this particular explosive, and the yellow always follows the green. He quickly twisted the green in place. Then, as his hand moved for the yellow, sweat dripped in his eye and blurred his vision. In the nick of time, he drew the yellow wire back and saw that he had almost connected it to the wrong terminal, which would have deactivated the bomb completely. His heart seemed to leap out of his chest, and he knew it must be beating 200 times a minute. After blinking several times to clear his vision, and after wiping the sweat from his forehead, he hooked up the yellow wire correctly.

One wire to go—with about 20 seconds left. Joe's heart raced, his forehead poured sweat, and his hands trembled. The next move he made could be his last. Had he connected the wires properly? If only he had paid more attention in class and been more serious during the training courses. He knew that his instructors had gone over this a thousand times, but there were so many different kinds of bombs and so many different wire sequences. How was he supposed to remember them all? All this thinking was costing him precious time. His time was down to 10 seconds. This could be the last 10 seconds of his life! The time ticked mercilessly—9...8...7...6...5...4— he had to hurry! Taking a deep breath and steadying his trembling hand, he put the blue wire to the last terminal, closed his eyes tightly, and gave it one final twist....

Maybe you think that life-and-death situations are only for guys in the movies or soldiers in the military. But that is not the case! Every day of your life you are making life-and-death decisions. In fact, the decisions that you make every day are more important than physical life and death. Your immortal soul is on the line, and your time on this Earth is ticking away. And just as it was important for Joe to connect the right wires to the right terminals, it is even more important for you to know exactly what you must do to secure a home in heaven. Playing a guessing game will never do. Who is willing to gamble with his or her soul? Your soul is far too important to risk by not knowing the exact "wires to connect."

Fortunately, your soul's salvation does not have to be a guessing game. On the contrary, God has given you everything you need so that you can know that eternal life awaits you. This book will help you discover which "wires to connect," so that as you make life's most important choices, you won't have to second-guess your decisions as a matter of doubt, but instead will be assured of them as...**a matter of fact**.

"So then faith comes by hearing, and hearing by the word of God."

Romans 10:17

Faith is not a leap into the unknown, but is a firm commitment based on what is known.

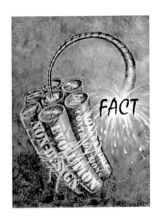

FAITH: FOUNDED ON FACTS

The doctor's office is crowded, as usual, when you walk in and find a seat. As you look through the magazines on the table, you find one that is mostly pictures and not too much writing. After thumbing through that one and three other magazines, the nurse finally steps through a door at the back of the room and calls out your last name. You follow her down a hall with several identical rooms on each side, and she directs you into one of them.

After waiting for what seems like hours, a middle-aged doctor wearing a white coat and a smile comes in, takes one of those flat, wooden sticks (also known as a tongue depressor), and nearly chokes you with it while trying to look down your throat. Then he listens to your heartbeat and looks in your ears. "Well," he says, "it looks like we are going to have to remove your spleen, one kidney, your tonsils, and a lung." You chuckle slightly, thinking that he is joking, but then you realize that he is serious.

Your eyes get as big as golf balls, and the blood drains from your face.

"But why doctor, I feel fine, what is wrong with me?"

The doctor looks you in the eye and says, "Nothing is wrong with you. Actually, you're in perfect health. But I **feel** like you need to have these things removed." Still very confused, you ask "Is there any evidence that these things are going to give me problems in the future?"

"Not much evidence" says the doc. "In fact, there is no rational reason. I just feel like it is the thing to do. You will have to trust me and take a leap of faith."

Now let's think seriously for a minute. Fortunately, this scenario would not happen in real life. But unfortunately, something very similar, yet much more serious, does often happen. Many religious people do not have any rational explanation for what they believe. When they are pressed to give a reason for their belief in God or Jesus, they say something like, "I can't give you any facts or evidence; you just have to believe it on faith." Is it true that having "faith" means accepting things to be true that you do not have the evidence to support?

Sadly, many people think this is what the Bible is talking about when it discusses faith. They think that biblical faith is "the power of believing what you can't prove to be true." Even *Webster's Dictionary* describes faith as a "firm belief in something for which there is no proof." One televangelist, Robert Schuller, said that "faith is a commitment to an unprovable assumption.... Both the atheist and the theist are making a commitment of faith. The atheist believes in nothing. The theist believes in something. But both are making a commitment to an unprovable assumption." If this view is correct, faith is based on a very small amount of truth, and is used by people as a crutch to fall back on when they have run out of evidence.

THE BIBLICAL VIEW OF FAITH

In truth, the biblical view of faith is not, and never has been, that of a "leap in the dark" or "a firm belief in something without proof." On the contrary, the biblical view of faith takes the exact opposite position. In the Bible, true faith rests on historical facts. The apostle Peter said that he and the other apostles "did not follow cunningly devised fables when we made known to you the power and coming of our Lord Jesus Christ, but were eyewitnesses of His majesty" (2 Peter 1:16). Peter very clearly stated that He had **proof** for his belief in Christ. Also, the apostle John made the same point when he wrote about "that which was from the beginning, which we have heard, which we have seen with our eyes, which we have looked upon, and our hands have handled" (1 John 1:1). The apostles never asked anyone to believe in Jesus without giving them solid, historical facts that could stand the test.

HOW DOES A PERSON
BUILD BIBLICAL FAITH?

The apostles of the Lord told us how they acquired much of their faith. It came by witnessing, firsthand, the miracles and resurrection of the Lord. In 1 Corinthians 15:4-9, the apostle Paul said that Jesus had been seen alive, after His death, by Peter and the rest of the apostles, including Paul himself. But the apostles were not the only ones to acquire faith by personally seeing Christ and His miracles. In John 4:42, several Samaritans came to the woman who had talked with Jesus at the well. They said to her: "Now we believe, not because of what you said, for we have heard for ourselves and know that this is indeed the Christ, the Savior of the world." Once again, these biblical characters saw Christ in the flesh and had firsthand evidence of His existence.

But what about us today? We have not seen Jesus perform miracles, we did not witness His resurrection, and we have not listened to Him preach a sermon. Can we ever have faith that is as strong as those people who personally saw, heard, and touched Jesus? The answer to that question is, "Yes, most definitely." Let's look at some ways to do that.

Faith Produced by Reliable Testimony

Have you personally been to China? Most of us have not. How sure are you that China actually exists—about 50%, 75%, 90%, or 100%? And what about that thing inside your head called a brain? Have you ever seen your own brain? How sure are you that there is one inside your head? And let's think about George Washington or Thomas Jefferson. Did you ever see either of these two men, talk to them, or hear them speak? How sure are you that they lived? The truth of the matter is, we are 100% sure that China exists, that we have a brain, and that George Washington and Thomas Jefferson existed—even though we have not personally seen, heard, or touched them. But, why are we so confident about these matters? Because we have accepted **reliable testimony** that verifies these facts. Now, let's see what the Bible says about that.

When Jesus rose from the grave on the first day of the week, He did not appear to all of His disciples at once. Mary Magdalene was one of the very first people to see Jesus after His resurrection (Mark 16:9-11). After she saw the Lord, she went to tell the other disciples that Jesus was alive. However, the Bible says that the other disciples "did not believe." A short time after this happened, Jesus appeared to two others who also went and told the disciples. But most of the disciples who had not seen Jesus did not believe them either (Mark 16:13). Should these disciples be commended for disbelieving, simply because they had not personally witnessed the resurrected Lord?

Jesus answered that question for us. In Mark 16:14 the Bible says: "Afterward He [Jesus] appeared to the eleven as they sat at the table; and He rebuked their unbelief and hardness of heart, because they did not believe those who had seen Him after He had risen." Jesus made it clear to His disciples, and to all of us who read the New Testament, that **reliable testimony provides evidence that can be used to build biblical faith.** This should not surprise us, when we consider the fact that testimony of eyewitnesses is used as evidence in courtrooms all across this country every day. Some people are sentenced to life in prison, others are released to go free, and still others receive the death penalty—all based on eyewitness testimony.

Even though personally witnessing something is one excellent way to verify facts, it certainly is not the **only** way. Reliable testimony, according to Jesus' standards, is another legitimate way of verifying a fact. That is exactly what the apostle Paul was saying in 2 Corinthians

5:7 when he remarked that "we walk by faith and not by sight." Many of the Corinthian Christians had not seen Jesus while he was on the Earth, yet they could still know that He existed. At one time in history, when Jesus lived in Palestine, faith was produced because of sight. But when Paul wrote to the Corinthians, and for us today, faith is produced not by sight, but by other equally valid means, one of which is reliable testimony.

Faith Produced by God's Revelation

Through eyewitness accounts from the apostles, we can build faith. But some things necessary for strong faith were not witnessed by the apostles or any other humans. For instance, no humans saw God make light on the first day of creation, and no one saw Him form the birds of the air or the fish of the sea. In some cases, reliable human testimony simply is not available. We must look to another source to build faith—God's revealed Word. The Bible has proven to be the most accurate book ever produced. Time and again it has been proven to be the inspired Word of God. Is it any wonder, then, that Romans 10:17 says: "So then faith comes by hearing, and hearing by the word of God." If reliable testimony is a valid way to verify facts, then what better source of reliable testimony could be provided than God Himself. God's inspired Word gives us His plan of salvation, His hatred of sin, and countless other things that cannot be learned from anyone but God Himself. When Jesus prayed, "Sanctify them by Your truth. Your word is truth," He meant exactly what He said. God's Word is truth. The reliable testimony and revelation found in that Word are effective tools that can be used to produce a faith founded on facts.

CONCLUSION

When the Bible speaks of having faith, it does not discuss a faith that is a "leap in the dark," or "a firm belief based on unprovable assumptions." In fact, the biblical idea of faith is exactly the opposite. Biblical faith is a firm belief in that which can be documented as true. It is based on such things as reliable testimony and the Word of God. Biblical faith says that we can **know** God exists (Psalm 46:10), we can **know** Jesus is His Son (1 John 5:20), we can **know** the Bible is His Word (2 Peter 1:20-21), and we can **know** that we are saved (1 John 5:13). Faith is not a leap into the unknown, but is a firm commitment based on what is known.

Suppose you leave your math homework assignment at school. You want to do it and make a good grade, but how are you going to know which problems to work? You have a decision to make. You could open your book and "guess" which problems to do based on which ones "feel" right, you could call a friend, or you could go back to school to get the assignment to make sure you do the right ones. When you get to math class the next day, which choice will you wish you had made?

In the same way, we can live this life "guessing" about Christianity and doing what "feels" right—taking "leaps in the dark" and following the world's idea of faith. Or, we can make sure we are doing right by going to the Bible to build our faith founded on facts. When the Day of Judgment comes, which choice will you wish you had made?

STUDY QUESTIONS

1. Give a definition of biblical faith.

2. How does biblical faith differ from the world's definition of faith?

3. How does the Bible tell us faith is produced?

4. What steps are you going to take to have a stronger biblical faith?

5. List some things other than the ones mentioned in this chapter that you know exist, even though you have never seen, tasted, touched, smelled, or heard them?

6. What is wrong with the idea that proof must always come through the five senses?

7. After reading 1 Peter 3:15, explain how the world's view of faith works against the instruction of this verse.

8. Look at 2 Peter 1:16-18 and Acts 1:3 and explain the point that these two biblical writers were making.

9. Read 1 Corinthians 2:12, 1 John 2:3,5, and 1 John 5:2,13. Do these verses sound like God wants you to be uncertain about your salvation?

10. Can you know for a fact that you are going to heaven? Are you going to heaven? If so, how do you know? If not, what are you going to do about it?

11. When God asks us to believe in Him, what are some of the evidences He gives us for that belief?

12. What were some of the evidences God gave the people in the Old Testament?

13. How will you show these evidences to other people?

"I will praise You, for I am fearfully and wonderfully made; marvelous are Your works, and that my soul knows very well."

Psalm 139:14

Design always demands a designer.

HIS FINGERPRINTS ARE EVERYWHERE

Sir Isaac Newton was a very famous mathematician and scientist who strongly believed in God. The story is told that he had an atheistic friend who did not believe in God. Sir Isaac devised a plan to try to convince his friend that God did exist and had created the Universe. One day, he went to a carpentry shop and asked the owner to make a model of our solar system. This model was to be to scale, intricately painted, and designed to resemble, as closely as possible, the actual solar system.

After several weeks, Isaac picked up the model, paid for it, and placed it in the center of a table in his house. Some time later, his atheist friend came over for a visit. When the friend arrived at Dr. Newton's house, the model of the solar system caught his eye, and he asked Sir Isaac if he could inspect the model more closely. Of course that was fine with Sir Isaac. As the atheist inspected the model, he was in awe of the fine craftsmanship and beauty of the pieces. After some time, the atheistic friend asked Isaac who had crafted this wonderful model of the solar system. Sir Isaac promptly replied that no one had made the model; it just appeared on his table by accident. Confused, the friend repeated the question, and yet Newton stubbornly clung to his answer that the model had just appeared "out of thin air." Finally, the friend became upset, and it was at that point that Isaac explained the purpose of his answer. If he could not convince his friend that this crude replica of the solar system had just happened by accident, how could the friend believe that the real solar system, with all its complexity and design, could have appeared just by time and chance? Point well taken! Design always demands a designer. Let's look at some intricate designs in this Universe that could not have happened by mere time and chance.

THE THOUGHT OF DESIGN

Inside your head is an organ that weighs about 3 pounds. Doctors who operate on this organ say that it feels like unbaked bread dough when you touch it or hold it in your hands. But this "doughy" organ we call the brain is certainly not a loaf of bread. On the contrary, it is the most complex "computer" the world has ever seen.

The brain is composed of over 10 trillion different cells. These cells work together to send electrical impulses at a rate of 273 miles per hour (393 feet per second). Nerve cells in the body send 2,000 impulses to the brain every second. These impulses come from 130,000 light receptors in the eye, 100,000 hearing receptors in the ears, 3,000 taste buds, and over 500,000 touch spots. As this is happening, the brain does not move, yet it consumes over 25% of the body's oxygen and receives 20% of all the blood that is pumped from the heart (which is pretty amazing, considering that the brain makes up only about 2% of the body weight of an average man).

And if all these "brainy" abilities don't impress you, consider that the brain serves as the "doctor" for the rest of the body. It produces more than 50 drugs, ranging from painkillers (like endorphin) to antidepressant drugs (like serotonin). In addition, the brain allows you to remember words, smells, pictures, and colors. In fact, the brain is so good at allowing a person to remember information, it would take 500 sets of encyclopedias to hold the information found in the brain. Let's be honest; if we were walking through the forest one day and found a laptop computer that weighed less than three pounds and yet could perform more complex tasks than any computer on the market, would we say it just "happened by accident?" If we use our brains, we can see that the design found in the brain demands an intelligent designer.

THE HEART OF DESIGN

Inside your body there are about 80,000 miles of arteries, blood vessels, veins, and capillaries, which make up a network that is longer than any single railroad system in the United States. Your heart (an organ about the size of a man's clenched fist) works hard every day to make sure that the proper amount of blood is distributed throughout the body. About 5 quarts of blood are pumped through the heart every minute (about 7,200 quarts every day). Yet, for all the pumping that your heart does, it rests about 6 hours each day. If you live to be 60, your heart will have rested almost twenty years. And it needs that rest, because it does enough work every minute to lift a 70-pound weight one foot off the ground. By the end of the day, your heart has done enough work to lift your body one mile straight into the air.

This mega-muscle beats about 75 times per minute in the average human. In a hundred-year period, it will have faithfully beaten 4 billion times and sent 600,000 tons of blood through the body. That blood makes a complete cycle from heart to the lungs, back to the heart, through the body, and then back to the heart in about one minute. And yet, some people expect us to believe that this efficient machine came about through random processes and blind chance.

If you compare an artificial heart (which took thousands of hours to design, millions of dollars to build, and hundreds of experiments to test) with a human heart, which is more efficient? Which would you rather have beating in your chest? Absolutely no question about it—humans have the heart of design!

TRAPPED BY DESIGN

When looking at the natural world of plants, one does not need to look very long until he or she can spot the fingerprints of God's design there as well. For instance, take the Venus' flytrap. If you are anything like the rest of us, the flytrap has always been a plant of interest to you. It is so intriguing because it does not get its nutrients solely from the ground and Sun like most plants. Instead, the Venus' flytrap has an intricate system that allows it to "eat" insects.

The plant grows to be about as tall as a 1-foot ruler. It has several hinged leaves that look just like a jaw; each one grows to be between 3-6 inches long. On the inside of these "jaws" are tiny "hairs" that grow. Also, the leaves have pointed, stiff bristles all along their edges. When an insect lands on a leaf, the tiny "hairs" detect the insect and the jaw snaps shut (all this takes less than half of a second). Immediately, the bristles on the edges lock together so that the insect cannot crawl out. Glands inside the leaves produce a special sap that begins to digest the insect. After about ten days, the insect is digested and the leaf opens back up, ready to strike again.

Just think of all the things in the Venus' flytrap that require design. The hinged leaves, the special sap, the pointed bristles, and the "hair" sensors all have to work together perfectly. All these special characteristics could not have just happened. They require a designer. If you were walking through the forest and your foot hit a trip line, the movement of the line triggered a trap door to open, you fell into a pit, the walls of the pit started closing in around you, and a gooey substance that could digest you started to pour out of holes in the wall, would you think it was just "an accident"? No? I wouldn't think so either.

SHOCKED BY DESIGN

The animal kingdom is another place God's design refuses to be hidden. Just look at the electric eel. The electric eel is not really an eel at all, but a fish. However, it is no ordinary fish. It is one of the most extraordinary fish in the entire world. It can grow to be 8 feet long and weigh up to 60 pounds. This fish breathes air and must come up to the surface of the water to take in big gulps. Also, this fish can produce 500-600 volts of static electricity within special cells underneath its skin (that is more than five times the punch that you would get by sticking your finger into an electrical socket).

In order for the electric eel to produce this "shocking" phenomenon, it must have a specially designed body. Its internal organs are all housed in the front 1/6 of the body. All along the slender body of the eel, highly compacted nerve endings connect to one another. Each nerve ending produces a small amount of electrical energy, but when they are added together, the combined power of the shock can stun or kill a human. Even more amazing is the fact that the eel never shocks itself, even though it is in water. It has a thick layer of fat that insulates it against its own (or other) electric shocks. Truly, the electric eel provides a marvelous example of design.

CONCLUSION

When people honestly survey all the wonders that surround them, it becomes increasingly difficult to deny that an intelligent Being had to have played a role in the creation of this world. The human brain, the human heart, the Venus' flytrap, and the electric eel are just a tiny sample of the amazing design in this Universe. Paul's words describing God ring just as true today as they did almost 2,000 years ago: "For since the creation of the world His invisible attributes are clearly seen, being understood by the things that are made" (Romans 1:20).

STUDY QUESTIONS

1. Read Romans 1:20 and Psalm 19:1-3. What argument are these two passages using to prove God's existence? How did Sir Isaac Newton use the same argument?

2. What characteristics does your brain share with a computer? Which (brain or computer) is the more efficient "machine"?

3. What are some things you can do that a computer will never be able to duplicate?

4. Natural hearts and brains are much better than those designed by humans. What does that say about the One Who designed them? Read 1 Corinthians 1:25 and Isaiah 55:9 and fit them into your discussion.

5. What is fascinating about the design of the Venus' Flytrap?

6. What interesting design does the electric eel have?

7. Why do you think God created such interesting animals and plants?

8. Did Sir Isaac Newton believe in creation or evolution? Was he an intelligent scientist? How does this relate to a Christian who wants to be a scientist today?

"...holy men of God spoke as they were moved by the Holy Spirit."

2 Peter 1:21

Although they were surrounded by false beliefs and practices, the biblical writers accurately prescribed medical practices and correctly presented scientific principles.

THE BIBLE IS STILL NUMBER ONE

Imagine trying to live in a world where every person decided for himself how long he thought one inch should be. One person's inch might be as long as a pencil, while another's might be as short as a matchstick. Further imagine trying to buy lumber or carpet, or trying to calculate any kind of geometry. In truth, trying to measure things without a standard is impossible.

The same is true for religion and spiritual things. If everyone were to make his own "measurements" about what is right and wrong, then mass confusion would rule the day. That is why God gave us the Bible. It is the standard by which all our actions should be measured. Because of the Bible's claim to be the only true standard, many have asked for evidence proving that it is from God. Such evidence is readily available—for the person who has an honest heart.

BACK TO THE FUTURE

A terrible tragedy shocked the United States when the World Trade Center and the Pentagon were attacked by terrorists on September 11, 2001. Amidst all of the horror, a rumor kept circulating that Nostradamus, a supposed fortuneteller, had predicted the turn of events. Web sites with Nostradamus information received thousands —even millions—of hits. After all was said and done, the rumored prediction turned out to have been fabricated and misunderstood; Nostradamus had no more predicted the future than you or I. But it was obvious from the public's response that anyone who can accurately predict the future is more than just a little special. The prophet Jeremiah said: "Who is he who speaks and it comes to pass, when the Lord has not commanded it?" (Lamentations 3:37). The prophet's point was clear: nobody accurately and consistently foretells the future unless God informs him of it. Therefore, when the Bible accurately predicts the future, we can know that it is from God.

"My God, My God, Why Have You Forsaken Me?"

If you were a Jew standing in the crowd watching Jesus hang on the cross, then you would have seen and heard many astonishing things. For one, you would have watched an innocent man being tortured, mocked, and spit upon. Also, you would have sat in complete darkness for three straight hours. But some of the most amazing things that happened on that day were the things Jesus said while on the cross.

As Jesus was nearing death, He cried out "Eloi, Eloi, lama sabachthani?," which means "My God, My God, why have you forsaken me?" Many of those around Jesus did not understand what He had said. Some thought He was calling for Elijah to come and help Him get off the cross. However, any Jew familiar with the Old Testament should have immediately recognized Jesus' statement as a direct quote from the first line of Psalm 22. King David wrote that psalm about 1,000 years before the death of Jesus. Yet verses 16 and 17 describe in minute detail what was happening at the crucifixion: "They pierced My hands and My feet; I can count all My bones. They look and stare at Me. They divide My garments among them, and for My clothing they cast lots."

Could you imagine having the 22nd Psalm in your hand (or mind) and watching the soldiers at Jesus' feet casting lots for His clothing (Matthew 27:35)? With one of Jesus' last breaths on the cross, He tried to get people to understand that He was the Messiah. And as we look upon the situation today, almost 2,000 years after the fact, He proved that the Bible had accurately foretold the future, proving it to be the inspired Word of God.

Call Him Out by His Name

Imagine taking a trip to Philadelphia, Pennsylvania, and visiting the State House where the Constitutional Convention took place in 1787. During the tour, your guide points to a document dating back to 1820. The piece of parchment tells of a man named George W. Bush from Austin, Texas, who would be President of the United States within the next 200 years. But how could someone know that a man named George W. Bush would be born in the United States? And how could someone know more than a century before Mr. Bush was ever born that he would be President of the United States? Furthermore, how could someone in 1820 know that a man from Texas (named George W. Bush) would be President of the United States when Texas wasn't even part of the Union yet? Such a prophecy truly would be amazing! Yet, obviously no such prediction was ever made.

One of the reasons we can **know** the Bible is from God is because it contains hundreds of prophecies about individuals, lands, and nations similar to the example above. One such prophecy was about a man named Cyrus, and two nations—Babylon and the Medo-Persian Empire. Isaiah vividly described how God would destroy the powerful kingdom of Babylon, "the glory of kingdoms" (13:19). Writing as if it had already occurred, Isaiah declared Babylon would fall (21:9). He then prophesied that Babylon would fall to the Medes and Persians (13; 21:1-10). Later, he proclaimed that the "golden city" (Babylon) would be conquered by a man named Cyrus (44:28; 45:1-7). This is a remarkable prophecy, especially since Cyrus was not even born until almost 150 years after Isaiah penned these words.

Isaiah not only predicted that Cyrus would overthrow Babylon, but he also wrote that Cyrus, serving as Jehovah's "anointed" and "shepherd," would release the Jews from captivity and assist them in their return to Jerusalem for the purpose of rebuilding the temple. All of this was written almost two hundred years before Cyrus conquered Babylon in 539 B.C. Amazing!

In case you're wondering about the factuality of this story, secular history verifies that all of these events came true. There really was a man named Cyrus who ruled the Medo-Persian Empire. He did conquer Babylon. And just as Isaiah prophesied, he assisted the Jews in their return to Jerusalem and in the rebuilding of the temple.

AMAZING FACTS OF LIFE

Many ancient cultures had ideas of science and medicine that were quite wrong. Some people in the past thought that a huge being named Atlas held the Earth on his massive shoulders. Others believed you could command the rain to fall by doing particular dances or magic spells. The ancient Egyptians believed that a mixture of worm blood and donkey dung cured splinters (bad news for the patients of those Egyptian doctors!).

Amazingly, the biblical writers did not make any of these errors in medicine and science. Although they were surrounded by false beliefs and practices, the biblical writers accurately prescribed medical practices and correctly presented scientific principles. How did the biblical writers consistently relay accurate medical practices and scientific facts? Some people have claimed that they "just got lucky." But if it was just luck, why did it happen so many times? A much better answer suggests that God inspired these writers and gave them accurate knowledge that they would have had no way of knowing on their own.

When to Operate

In Genesis 17:12, God commanded Abraham to circumcise all newborn males on the eighth day after they were born. But what is so important about the eighth day?

Wouldn't the seventh or ninth have been just as good as the eighth? Actually, the eighth day is extremely important because in humans, blood clotting depends upon three key factors: (a) platelets; (b) vitamin K; and (c) prothrombin.

Interestingly, it is only on the fifth to seventh days of a newborn baby's life that vitamin K is present in adequate quantities. Obviously, then, if vitamin K is not produced in sufficient quantities until days five through seven, it would be wise to postpone any surgery until sometime after that. But why did God specify day **eight**?

On the eighth day, the amount of prothrombin is **elevated above 100 percent of normal**. In fact, day eight is the only day in the male's life in which this will be the case under normal conditions. If surgery is to be performed, day eight is the perfect day to do it. We know these facts today because we have been able to study thousands of babies over many years, but Abraham had no such research methods. How did he know that the eighth day was the perfect day to perform any type of surgery? One reason presents itself: God revealed this knowledge to Abraham.

Pass on the Pig

If you have been around your mother when she cooked pork chops or bacon, then she probably has told you to wash your hands after touching any of the plates or containers where the raw pork has been. She wants you to wash your hands because she understands that raw or undercooked pork can cause disease. But thousands of years before your mother's hand-washing instructions, God was protecting His children from the same diseases.

In the Old Testament, God allowed the children of Israel to eat only certain kinds of meat. Among land animals, only those that had a split hoof and chewed the cud could be eaten (Leviticus 11:3). Of the water-living animals, only those with fins and scales were acceptable (Leviticus 11:9; of interest is the fact that poisonous fish have no scales). But perhaps the best known among these biblical restrictions was eating the meat of a pig. To the Jew, pork was considered unclean and could not be eaten under any circumstance.

You see, the pig is a scavenger, like a buzzard, and will eat almost anything. Because of this, pigs occasionally eat the parasite *Trichinella spiralis*, which is the cause of trichinosis in humans. Left untreated, this disease can be very serious and even deadly. Pigs also are known carriers of tapeworms and other parasites that cause tumors in the liver, lungs, and other parts of the body. Raw or undercooked pork can be quite dangerous when eaten by humans. Pigs can provide safe meat if they are fed properly and cooked correctly. But such conditions often were not present in ancient times.

Were the Israelites "ahead of their times" in regard to their extensive public health and personal hygiene laws? Archaeologists admit that they have yet to find civilizations as ancient as the Israelites with rules and regulations that could compare to those of the Jewish people in regard to scientific accuracy. Interestingly, even today in some countries (like Germany) raw pork is considered a delicacy—in spite of the knowledge we possess about the potential dangers of eating it.

CONCLUSION

Predictive prophecy and scientific foreknowledge (such as when to circumcise, what not to eat, etc.) fill the pages of the Bible, giving solid evidence to prove that the Bible is the Word of God. As such, the Bible provides the only "measuring stick" that people should use to determine how to live their lives. Truly, the Bible is no work of human genius; on the contrary, "holy men of God spoke as they were moved by the Holy Spirit" (2 Peter 1:20-21).

Now the question becomes: What are you doing with the Bible? Many of us know that the Bible is inspired, but we leave it on our shelves to collect dust. George Gallup (the man behind the Gallup Polls) stated that the Bible is the most respected book in America—and the least read! Let us not be like those people described in Hosea 4:6 who were "destroyed for lack of knowledge." Instead, let's be like the noble Bereans who "searched the scriptures daily" (Acts 17:11).

STUDY QUESTIONS

1. What is predictive prophecy?

2. What is scientific foreknowledge?

3. How can these things be used to prove the inspiration of the Bible?

4. Discuss some other prophecies or examples of scientific foreknowledge that were not listed in the chapter (read Micah 5:2, Numbers 19:11, and Isaiah 53).

5. Psalm 22:16-17 is a messianic prophecy. What is a messianic prophecy? What were these prophecies designed to do?

6. Do you think if you had been an Israelite growing up under the Old Law, you would have studied enough to recognize the Messiah when He came? What kept many people from recognizing Christ as the Messiah? What keeps people from following Him today?

7. Why did God give the children of Israel rules about when to operate on male children and what kinds of food to eat (read Exodus 15:26 and Deuteronomy 8:1)?

8. Why do you think God makes rules for us today about things like sex and drinking alcohol (1 Corinthians 6:18; Ephesians 5:18)?

9. Discuss what happens in religion when people decide to follow God in ways that "feel right" to them yet go against the Bible (read Judges 21:25 and Jeremiah 10:23). What is the solution to this problem?

"What do these stones mean to you?"

Joshua 4:6

The more we uncover the past, the more we uncover the truth—the Bible is indeed the Word of God.

ARCHAEOLOGY—
BURIED TREASURE

A man with a leather vest and a broad-rimmed hat wraps a torn piece of cloth around an old bone, sets it on fire, and uses it as a torch to see his way through ancient tunnels filled with bones, rats, bugs, and buried treasure. Close behind him lurks the dastardly villain ready to pounce on the treasure after the hero has done all the planning and dangerous work. We have seen this scenario, and others very similar to it, time and again in movies like *Indiana Jones* or *The Mummy*. And although we understand that Hollywood exaggerates and dramatizes the situation, it still remains a fact that finding ancient artifacts excites both young and old alike. How many of us have wanted a metal detector so that we could dig up old Civil War bullets or find ancient coins that we "knew" would be worth thousands of dollars? How many of us have ever searched for arrowheads left by mysterious Indian civilizations?

Finding things left by people of the past is exciting because a little window of their lives is opened to us. When we find an arrowhead, we learn that the Indians used bows and arrows to hunt and fight. Discovering a piece of pottery tells us how the ancients cooked or drew water from wells. Every tiny artifact gives the modern person a more complete view of life in the past.

Because of the importance of archaeology, many have turned to it in order to answer certain questions about the past. One of the questions most often asked is, "Did the things recorded in the Bible really happen?" Truth be told, archaeology cannot always answer that question. Nothing material remains from Elijah's trip in the fiery chariot, and no physical artifacts exist to show that Christ actually walked on water. Therefore, if we ask archaeology to "prove" that the entire Bible is true or false, we are faced with the fact that archaeology can neither prove nor disprove the Bible's validity. However, even though it cannot prove the Bible's validity by itself, it does provide an important source of evidence that can be combined with other facts to prove the validity of the Scriptures. Let's dig through the evidence and see what buried treasures have been uncovered.

HITTITES—WHERE ARE YOU?

Almost 50 times in the Old Testament we read about a people known as the Hittites. They were major players in Jewish history and were listed as one of the nations that the children of Israel needed to conquer when entering the Promised Land (Joshua 11:3-4). Also, King David had among his army a valiant Hittite named Uriah, who was murdered upon David's command because the king had committed adultery with his wife, Bathsheba. Without a doubt, the Old Testament frequently mentions the Hittites as a very real nation. But for many years, in secular history and archaeology the Hittites were as invisible as men from Mars. No solid archaeological evidence could be found that verified the existence of the Hittites. For this reason, certain critics laughed at the biblical record, and insisted that the absence of information on the Hittites showed that the Bible was filled with phony historical references.

However, the year 1876 saw many people changing their minds about the Hittites and the Bible. An archaeologist named Hugo Winckler visited a city in Turkey named Boghaz-Köy. Upon digging up portions of the city, he found a breathtaking amount of human artifacts—including five temples, many sculptures, and a fortified castle. But more important, he found a huge storeroom filled with over 10,000 clay tablets. After completing the difficult task of deciphering the tablets, it was announced to the world that the Hittites had been found. The sight at Boghaz-Köy had been the Hittite capital city named Hattusha.[1]

All the people who had used the absence of archaeological evidence about the Hittites to mock the Bible's accuracy were shamefaced and silent, while another small piece of evidence was added to the ever-growing mass of facts verifying the Bible's accuracy.

PILATE—LOST AND FOUND

The last few days of Jesus' life were the most tragic of any in human history. Ruthless men and women mocked Him, spit upon Him, and even bit Him. Amidst all the violence, there stood one man who had the power to stop all the torture—one man who could call off the Roman soldiers and save Christ from being crucified. His name was Pontius Pilate, the Roman official who governed the area of Judea at the time of Christ's death. The story of the crucifixion can hardly be told without mentioning the name of this Roman official who sentenced Christ to death—even though Pilate knew Jesus was innocent.

But even though the Bible mentions Pilate on several occasions, his name could not be found among the archaeological evidence. For hundreds of years, no stone inscriptions or other physical proof could be produced to support the idea that a man named Pilate had anything to do with Christ. Because of this, some mocked the Bible and claimed that creative biblical writers concocted Pilate from their imaginations. After all, if Pilate were such a prominent leader, wouldn't there be some kind of archaeological evidence to verify his existence?

Once again, however, the critics were silenced. In 1961, a team of Italian archaeologists working at Caesarea found a stone tablet that measured 32 inches high, by 27 inches wide, by 8 inches thick. On this slab were the remains of this simple inscription "Pontius Pilate, Prefect of Judea"—almost the exact same title as the one given to him in Luke 3:1. This, then, became yet another find to remind us that the more we uncover the past, the more we uncover the truth—the Bible is indeed the Word of God.

"OF THE HOUSE OF DAVID"

Of all the men in the Old Testament, few are spoken of with such reverence and honor as King David—shepherd, psalmist, soldier, and king. With God's mighty power behind him, he slew a bear and a lion to save his father's sheep, toppled a wicked giant with a single stone, defeated thousands of godless Philistines, and united the children of Israel under a throne of righteousness and justice. The Bible mentions David approximately 1,000 times. He wrote 73 of the psalms, and stands as the major character in at least 62 chapters of the Old Testament. Anyone who has ever read the Good Book cannot help but know the name of David—a man said to be "after God's own heart" (1 Samuel 13:14). Those familiar with the modern-day nation of Israel know that its flag proudly bears a symbol known as the Star of David.

Yet, if the Bible is removed from the discussion, David—King of Israel—vanishes into the shadows of secular history. At least he did for almost 3,000 years. David's name and story were clearly missing from archaeological evidence. His name was so absent, in fact, that for many years, skeptics called David's life a fantasy and referred to his deeds as mere legends. After all, every nation needs a hero who slays giants. The Saxons had Beowulf, the Greeks had Hercules, and the Jews had David. David's daring deeds and courageous conduct were relegated to the relic heaps of myth.

But something discovered in Palestine in 1993 changed David's status in secular history forever. Professor Avraham Biran, director of the Nelson Glueck School of Biblical Archaeology at Hebrew Union College, was digging at a site in northern Israel known as Tel Dan. There he unearthed a 3,000-year-old black basalt stone inscribed by one of the enemies of the ancient nation of Israel. The stone explained that Ben Hadad, King of Damascus, had defeated the Israelites and taken many of them captive. But perhaps the most amazing aspect of the stone is that it plainly states that the Israelite king defeated by Ben Hadad was "of the house of David." The Bible uses the exact same term several times (read 1 Kings 12:19; 14:8; Isaiah 7:2). For the first time in secular history, the name of David appeared connected to Israel. The implications of the stone cannot be ignored. If a king—any king—had reigned and belonged to the "house of David," then there must have been a real, historical David who established such a house.[2]

Because of this find, the story of David has assumed a new place in the halls of history. No longer can David, King of Israel, be relegated to the status of myth or legend. Instead, he takes his rightful place beside the other documented kings of ancient history. David lived, just as the Bible had stated. And once again, the Bible and archaeological fact stand side by side.

CONCLUSION

We have examined only a tiny portion of the archaeological evidence in this chapter. Yet it is enough to show that the Bible and archaeological facts fit together like pieces of a jigsaw puzzle. One of the most famous archaeologists of his time, Nelson Glueck, said it like this: "No archaeological discovery has ever controverted (gone against—KB) a Biblical reference. Scores of archaeological findings have been made which confirm in clear outline or exact detail historical statements in the Bible."

Yes, the archaeological evidence confirms the Bible on countless occasions, providing even more evidence to document that it is the inspired Word of God. As such, we must go to that Word for the answers to problems in our lives, since it is "living and powerful" (Hebrews 4:12). God can transform us from guilt-plagued sinners into strong, faithful Christians if we will be obedient to His Word. But such a change will not happen by accident. The words of the Bible will not "seep" into our minds by putting it under our pillows while we sleep. We must be like the prophet Ezra who "had prepared his heart to seek the Law of the Lord, and to do it" (Ezra 7:10).

REFERENCES

[1] Price, Randall (1997), *The Stones Cry Out* (Eugene, OR: Harvest House), page 83.

[2] see footnote above, pages 161-174.

STUDY QUESTIONS

1. What are some things that archaeology can show us?

2. What are some things that it cannot tell us?

3. Can archaeology fully prove the Bible's inspiration? Why or why not? What can it prove about the Bible?

4. Besides verifying the accuracy of the Bible, how else can archaeology help us understand the Bible?

5. What would you like to know about the ways of life in the first century?

6. Judging from the examples given, do Bible critics generally insult the Bible because they have not found what they think they should, or because they have found something that they think goes against the Bible? Why is that significant? How could the principles found in James 1:19 and Proverbs 18:13 apply to this problem?

7. What do you think future archaeological finds will tell about the Bible?

8. If archaeology continues to verify the biblical account, will that satisfy most Bible critics? Why or why not? Fit John 12:37 into your answer.

9. If you are not yet convinced that the Bible is God's Word, what evidence would convince you that it is?

10. If you are convinced that it is God's Word, what are you doing with it? What steps are you taking to "prepare your heart to seek the Law of the Lord?"

"For we are not writing any other things to you than what you read or understand. Now I trust you will understand, even to the end."

2 Corinthians 1:13

Make no mistake about it; God in-spired the Bible in a way that humans can understand it.

UNDERSTANDING THE BIBLE

Take a short drive through any city in the United States, and you will probably see more church buildings than you can count on your fingers and toes combined. Let your fingers take a walk through the nearest phone book, and the numbers may reach into the thousands. It is interesting that most of these different churches claim to be using the Bible as the book that guides their teachings and practices. With all these different beliefs supposedly coming from the Bible, one wonders if it is possible to understand the Bible at all? Many atheists claim that the Bible is a confusing book filled with contradictions and lies that make it impossible to understand or believe. In fact, one critic said that the Bible is "a book that is so unintelligible that not only do 'non-believers' reject it, but those who believe it to be the true word of God cannot agree upon its interpretation."

One thing is for sure: many of those who believe the Bible to be the Word of God cannot agree upon its interpretation. But the reason they cannot agree upon its meaning is not because the Bible is an "unintelligible" book. There are many reasons why people misunderstand the Bible and disagree about its meaning. Examining some of them can help each of us understand the Bible better.

CAN IT BE UNDERSTOOD?

Some people think that, since the Bible is the Word of God, then it is too "lofty" to be understood. They think that no human can understand God's Word, and therefore it is pointless to attempt such an achievement. But this idea goes directly against what the Word of God actually says. In 2 Corinthians 1:13, the apostle Paul wrote: "For we are not writing any other things to you than what you read or understand. Now I trust you will understand, even to the end." His point could not have been clearer —the words of the apostle's letter (and of the entire Bible for that matter) are understandable. The book of Ephesians makes a similar statement: "Therefore do not be unwise, but understand what the will of the Lord is" (5:17). Make no mistake about it; God inspired the Bible in a way that humans can understand it (which would make perfect sense if He wanted to communicate with His creation).

THE BIBLE IS RESPECTED, BUT NOT READ

One major reason people do not understand the Bible is because many of them spend very little time reading it. The Gallup polling organization surveyed many

U.S. citizens and asked them some basic Bible questions. The results of the survey show the degree of biblical ignorance in our country today. Six out of ten Americans could not say for sure who gave the Sermon on the Mount. At least 50% of those polled could not name the four gospels of the New Testament. Fewer than half could name Genesis as the first book in the Bible. Eight out of every ten Americans believed the Bible says, "God helps those who help themselves." And 12% of those polled thought that Joan of Arc was Noah's wife!

Is it any wonder that such disagreement about the Bible exists in our society today? Very few people are reading The Book, but still they claim to know and believe what it says. It is like a game of Monopoly® where people sit around and argue about the rules, yet never bother to read the actual rule book. Should we expect anything but confusion and misunderstanding from such a situation?

As simple as it may sound, reading the Bible is the only way to understand it. The apostle Paul told the Ephesians: "When you read, you may understand my knowledge in the mystery of Christ" (3:4). He also encouraged the young preacher Timothy to "give attention to reading" (1 Timothy 4:13). Nothing clears up misunderstanding about the Bible better than simply reading it.

CONTEXT MATTERS—*REALLY* MATTERS

In your younger years of school, one of the first language skills you learned was to use context clues to help you solve problems or understand the meanings of words. For instance, what does the word "bear" mean? It could be a noun referring to a big, furry mammal with large teeth. Or maybe it is being used in its verbal form, meaning "to endure." Only context can give you the meaning of the word. Read the two sentences and decide which meaning goes with each sentence.

> The **bear** jumped into the water after a salmon.

> God will provide a way of escape so that you can **bear** temptation.

Obviously, the first sentence is talking about an animal, while the word in the second sentence means "to endure." That was easy to figure out, but it could be done only by using the context.

In the same way, the Bible puts things in context, and that context must be used to understand what is being said. For instance, in the book of Job the Bible says to "curse God" (2:9). That is a very disturbing thought. We know that in other places, the Bible says that we should love, honor, and serve God as our Creator. So which is it? Should we honor and serve Him, or should we curse Him? The answer is easy to find if we look at the context of the verse in Job. Job had just lost his most precious worldly possessions— children, health, and riches. As he sat in the middle of an ash heap scraping his boils with a broken piece of pottery, his wife looked upon him with sorrow, because she wanted Job's pain to end. This is what she said to Job: "Do you still hold to your integrity? Curse God and die!" When Job heard this advice, he was troubled and said to her, "You speak as one of the foolish women speaks. Shall we indeed accept good from God, and shall we not accept adversity?" Obviously, once the context is taken into account, the Bible does not tell anyone that cursing God is a good thing to do. Job's wife mistakenly commented that Job should curse God, and Job corrected her. Context matters—**really** matters!

FIGURES OF SPEECH

Suppose your little brother volunteers to bring you a soda from the refrigerator. On his return, he slips on a rug and accidentally throws your beverage across the room. Witnessing the sight, you comment, "Smooth move, little brother." Did you really mean that your little brother was graceful and smooth? Of course not. You meant the exact opposite, and used a figure of speech known as sarcasm to get your point across. It may come as a surprise to you, but the Bible does the same thing.

In the book of 2 Corinthians, some of the Christians were accusing Paul of treating them badly. Many times throughout the book he explained that never once had he treated them unjustly. In chapter 12:13, he said: "For what is it in which you were inferior to other churches, except that I myself was not burdensome to you? Forgive me this wrong!" Was the apostle really asking for forgiveness for not being burdensome to the Corinthian church? No, he was using sarcasm to make the point that he had never mistreated the church at Corinth.

Throughout the Bible, many different figures of speech are used; sarcasm is just one of them. Let's look at another one called hyperbole. Hyperbole is simply the exaggeration of facts to make a point. If you were invited to a party and someone said that "everybody" was going to be there, that person would be using hyperbole. It is impossible for "everybody" in the world to be at the party. Yet, you would not call your friend a liar because he or she used such terminology, because you understand the figure of speech being used. The Bible does the same thing. Take John 4:39 as an example. In this passage, a Samaritan woman speaks of Jesus and says, "He told me **all** that I ever did." Had Jesus really told that woman **everything** that she had ever done in her life? No, she was using hyperbole to make her point. Hyperbole is one of the more common figures of speech in the Bible.

Figurative Language

When people speak literally, they mean exactly what they say. If I say that I own a car, then I mean that I own a car. But there are times when a person speaks figuratively and not literally. When a person uses figurative language, then that person uses words to symbolize something else. For instance, when a person says, "That politician is a snake," he or she does not literally mean that the politician is a reptile that crawls around on its belly. The point is that the politician is sneaky or sly.

Many of the biblical writers used figurative language. In Luke 13:32, Jesus had been warned that King Herod was trying to kill Him. Jesus replied by saying, "Go, tell that fox...." Did Jesus really mean that Herod was a furry animal about the size of a small dog with a bushy tale? Absolutely not. He did mean, however, that Herod was a sly, sneaky fellow.

Again, in John 10:9 when Jesus spoke about a place where shepherds kept their sheep, He called Himself "the door" of the sheepfold. Did He mean that He was a tall piece of wood with a knob and hinges? No. He simply meant that everyone must go through Him to get to the Father. Jesus often used figurative language.

The book of Revelation is filled with figurative language. If a person does not understand figurative language, then it would be impossible to understand the book of Revelation. It would be like my saying that my dog "kicked the bucket." You would understand that I mean my dog died. But what if my statement were buried for 2,000 years and then read by people in the future who did not use or understand the phrase "kicked the bucket." Would they think I had owned a special "kicking" dog? Figurative language plays an important role in the Bible.

LET'S BE HONEST

Many people "misunderstand" the Bible because it teaches things they do not want to obey. Instead of changing their sinful lives, they decide to twist the Bible to say what they want it to say. This could be the major reason why the Bible is "misunderstood." The apostle Peter described this situation by saying that some untaught and unstable people take the Scriptures and twist them "to their own destruction" (2 Peter 3:16). Being honest with the Bible, instead of trying to force it to agree with our lives, will help us to understand it better.

Thomas Jefferson, the third president of the United States, did not believe in miracles, so he literally cut out the parts of the New Testament that spoke of miracles. Many people today do the same thing. If they don't like a passage for one reason or another, they cut it out or change it to fit their lifestyle, instead of changing their lifestyle to fit the Bible.

CONCLUSION

In this chapter, we have looked at just a few reasons why people often misunderstand God's Word. Some claim that it cannot be understood, others neglect to look at the context of particular passages, and still others do not recognize the figures of speech being used in the Bible. Many try to twist it to fit their sinful lives. And still others do not even read it. How can we understand the Bible, avoid these pitfalls, and help bring unity to the Lord's church? By obeying the words of Paul to the young preacher Timothy when he said: "Be diligent to present yourself approved to God, a worker who does not need to be ashamed, rightly dividing the word of truth" (2 Timothy 2:15).

STUDY QUESTIONS

1. What are some reasons that people misunderstand the Bible?

2. What are some ways that those misunderstandings can be resolved?

3. Do you always understand the Bible?

4. What do you think are the main reasons for your personal misunderstandings?

5. How can you work to improve your understanding of the Bible (be specific)?

6. Does God want you to misunderstand the Bible? Explain how 1 Corinthians 14:33 and James 3:16 fit into this discussion.

7. What does Hebrews 5:12 tells us about solving confusion?

8. Read John 6:27 and 2 Thessalonians 3:10. What potential misunderstanding might arise between these two verses? How can it be solved? What about Matthew 7:1 and John 7:24?

9. What figure of speech is being used in John 12:19? In 1 Kings 10:27? In Luke 13:33? In Revelation 1:16 (read Ephesians 6:17 for help with this verse)?

"Where is the wise? Where is the scribe? Where is the disputer of this age? Has not God made foolish the wisdom of this world?"

1 Corinthians 1:20

There is not a grain of truth to the notion that most people believe in evolution, or that all "educated" people hold to it as a fact.

EVOLUTION—A THEORY
FALLING ON HARD TIMES

For the past twenty years, creation has rarely been taught in the public school system. The Bible practically has been banned from the classroom, and textbooks promoting the theory of evolution have taken over. Chances are, if you do not attend a private school that teaches Bible, then you have never been taught in any type of science class about the many facts that disagree with the theory of evolution and support the concept of creation. It is a shame that we often are forced to use "Bible class" time to study science, but we must. If we do not, some of you might end up in a high school or college class being confronted with the theory of evolution, having never seen the evidence against it.

Even though many people have tried to keep that evidence from you, it refuses to be silenced. In fact, as much as some evolutionists hate to admit it, twenty years of evolutionary teaching have not convinced the majority of Americans to believe the theory. For example, a 1997 Gallup poll found that 44% of Americans believed in a fairly literal reading of the Genesis story of creation. The same poll found that another 39% believed that God played some part in creation (that's a total of 73% who believed that God played some part in creation). Only 10% believed in a purely evolutionary origin of the Universe. Two years later, in a similar poll in 1999, 47% of the people questioned believed in a recent creation of man, and only 9% believed in naturalistic evolution. Evolution is not "generally accepted as fact" by most people. On the contrary, most people accept creation as the true account of our origin.

Contrary to what some people believe, it is not the "ignorant" majority who believe in creation and the "elite" minority who believe in evolution. Some of the most brilliant men ever to have lived believed in a recent creation. Take Isaac Newton for example (the scientist who explained the laws of gravity). He once said that he believed "in the Bible as the word of God." Lord Kelvin is another good example. He played a major role in the development of modern physics, published hundreds of scientific papers, and held 70 patents on his own inventions. He once stated that "overwhelmingly strong proofs of intelligent and benevolent design lie around us . . . the atheistic idea is so non-sensical that I cannot put it into words." The list could go on and on: Samuel Morse (who invented Morse Code), George Washington Carver (who invented peanut butter), and Wernher von Braun (a leader in U.S. space technology in his day) are just a few examples of intelligent men who believed in creation.

These brilliant men of the past are accompanied by just as many intellectual minds in the present. Maybe you have heard of a medical device that performs what is known as an MRI (Magnetic Resonance Imaging, where high-quality images of the inside of the body are produced)? One of its main inventors was Dr. Raymond Damadian, a strong believer in creation. In fact, institutions such as the Creation Research Society in Missouri or the Institute for Creation Research in California are composed of hundreds of scientists who hold advanced degrees and who believe strongly in creation.[1] There is not a grain of truth to the notion that most people believe in evolution, or that all "educated" people hold to it as a fact.

Those who believe in creation have seen the serious problems involved in the theory of evolution. Let's look at a few of those problems in this chapter.

NATURAL SELECTION

The Origin of Species by Means of Natural Selection was the title of Charles Darwin's book, first published in 1859. Those last two words, "natural selection," have been discussed often in the halls of science. And it is no secret that Darwin's concept of natural selection (or "survival of the fittest," as it has come to be known) has been at the center of evolutionary thought.

According to Darwin, a creature with a particular advantage—the "fittest of its kind"—would be naturally selected to pass on the advantage to its offspring. A horse with long legs, for example, would be able to gallop faster than the rest, thus escaping from wolves or other predators in order to produce heirs. A "fit" creature, therefore, was one that could best carry out the functions that kept it alive and was best adapted to its environment. This is what Darwin meant by "survival of the fittest."

But problems with the theory of natural selection soon developed. Somehow, natural selection was supposed to ensure the "survival of the fittest," but the only realistic way to define the "fittest" was "those that survive." Basically, then, natural selection simply says that all the winners win, and those who win are the winners. Natural selection does not explain how those creatures came to be the most "fit."

Creationists have never objected to the idea of natural selection as a mechanism for eliminating unfit, poorly adapted organisms. As a matter of fact, creationists long before Darwin said that natural selection was a good conservation principle (think of it as a screening device for getting rid of the unfit). If a harmful mutation causes a grasshopper to have only one leg, then that grasshopper will be an easier meal for a bird. Natural selection is the Creator's plan for preventing harmful mutations from destroying an entire species. But natural selection cannot cause one kind of animal or plant to "evolve" into another kind of animal or plant. In reality, it is nothing more than an argument that reasons in a circle. As one scientist said, "natural selection can account for the **survival** of the fittest, but it cannot account for the **arrival** of fittest."

GENETIC MUTATIONS

At the turn of the century, just as Darwin's idea of natural selection was beginning to fall on hard times, the science of genetics was born. Some who began to study genetics felt that they had found the actual mechanism of evolution—genetic mutations. The new idea then became that species arose by mutations that (somehow) were plugged into the system by natural selection. Today the supposed mechanism of evolution is natural selection **plus** genetic mutations (since natural selection by itself has no power to create anything).

Evolution without a mechanism is like a car with no engine—it is not going anywhere. Evolutionists soon realized that natural selection **alone** was not a sufficient mechanism. Organisms would not (and could not!) change from one species to another unless the genetic material was changed. Mutations are genetic changes passed from parent to offspring.

The only possible mechanism of evolution is natural selection plus genetic mutations. We are told that "nature" has "selected" certain beneficial mutations and plugged them into various organisms, eventually causing those organisms to change from one kind to another. But there are some very serious problems with this idea. Consider, for example, the following.

1. **Mutations are random.** There is no way to control mutations or to predict with accuracy when they will occur. In other words, nature is not "selecting" at all. Rather, "nature" is forced to accept whatever appears. The obvious question, then, is: What appears?

2. **Mutations are very rare.** How often do random mutations occur? One scientist said: "It is probably fair to estimate the frequency of a majority of mutations in higher organisms between **one in ten thousand and one in a million** per gene per generation." Evolutionists themselves frankly admit what every research biologist knows: mutations occur rarely, and when they do, they are entirely random.

3. **Good mutations are very, very rare.** In theory, there are at least three kinds of mutations: good, bad, and neutral. Obviously, the bad mutations (causing various diseases and death) are not what the evolutionist needs. Neutral mutations are of little use as well, since they are neither harmful nor helpful. So the question really is: How often do **good** mutations occur? Hermann J. Muller, an award-winning scientist in the field of genetics, said: "Accordingly, the great majority of mutations, certainly well over 99%, are harmful in some way, as is to be expected of the effects of accidental occurrences."

What conclusion can be drawn from these facts? The famous evolutionist George Gaylord Simpson of Harvard University admitted that if there were a population of 100 million individuals, and they produced a new generation every day, the likelihood of obtaining good evolutionary results from mutations could be expected once every **274 billion years!** He therefore was forced to conclude: "Unless there is an unknown factor tremendously increasing the chance of simultaneous mutations, such a process has played no part whatever in evolution." Mutations are mostly destructive, and cannot provide a reasonable answer for evolution. Furthermore, mutations simply change something that already exists. Mutations do not create anything new, but only alter what is already present. Mutations can cause a fly to have six wings, a fish to have three eyes, or a person to have an abnormal face, but they cannot create a fly or fish or person—no matter how much time is available. Natural selection plus mutations still does not answer the question of life's origin and development.

CONCLUSION

If it has not happened to you yet, it will in the future. Solid evidence against evolution will be withheld from you in the classroom, on educational television, or in the textbooks. You will be told that only uneducated, ignorant people believe in creation. In fact, you might even be turned down from certain schools, lose a job, or be ridiculed for believing in creation. But think about it: if evolution is such a strong theory that has so much factual support, why won't educators let other ideas such as creation be presented along with of evolution. Is it because they know that the true facts of science support creation? You deserve better than to have the truth withheld from you. You deserve to know **all** the facts. Take it upon yourself to find the truth.

REFERENCES

[1] Perloff, James (1999), *Tornado in a Junkyard* (Arlington, MA: Refuge Books), pages 237-251.

STUDY QUESTIONS

1. According to the Gallup polls mentioned in this chapter, how many Americans believe in strict evolution?

2. How many believe in a recent creation? Which category best describes your belief?

3. Before you read these poll results, what percentages would you have guessed?

4. It has been said that only "dumb" people believe in creation and that all the "smart folks" believe in evolution. What would you say to that?

5. Who are some brilliant men that believe(d) in creation, and what accomplishments did those men achieve?

6. Charles Darwin believed that natural selection was responsible for evolution. What problems were soon discovered with this idea?

7. What are some things natural selection cannot do?

8. Do creationists deny the idea of natural selection? If not, what part do creationists say natural selection plays in nature?

9. As problems with Darwin's idea of natural selection developed, what new mechanism was supposed to account for evolution? What are some of the major problems associated with this new theory?

10. What can mutations do? What can they not do?

11. Where should you be learning these scientific facts? Why aren't you learning them there?

12. What do you think will happen in the future if people try to teach these things in public schools?

13. Are these things any "less scientific" than other topics that favor evolution? Explain your answer.

"You, Lord, in the beginning laid the foundation of the earth, and the heavens are the work of Your hands. They will perish, but You remain; and they will all grow old like a garment."

Hebrews 1:10-11

When the cold, hard facts are placed on the table, the proven scientific laws of thermodynamics disprove the theory of evolution and verify the idea of Creation.

NOT MAKING PROGRESS

One sure way to let something ruin is simply to do nothing to take care of it. Everyone knows that a brand new car left untouched in a driveway for twenty years will not look better at the end of that period of time. No one would claim that a toy truck left in the sandbox by a three-year-old is going to look newer after six months of weathering. If your room is dirty, do you think that it will clean itself if you leave it alone for three months? Of course you don't! Neglecting your room will only give it more time to collect dust.

Every time we see things wearing down over time, we are witnessing a scientific law. What is a scientific law? A scientific law is a principle in nature that is true in every observable case. Whether the measurements come from the sunny islands of Hawaii or the ice-covered tundra of the Arctic, a scientific law is the same for all places. But one thing we must remember about scientific laws is that scientists **do not make the laws, they only observe them and label them.** For instance, one scientific law is the Law of Biogenesis. This law says that all life originates from previous life of its own kind. That means that a cow produces a baby calf, and a chicken gives birth to a chick. While it is true that scientists put the law in understandable terms, it is also true that cows were giving birth to calves long before science decided to label the process as a law. Scientific laws occur regardless of whether we humans like them or not. If you are standing beneath a building and someone drops a bowling ball from the top, the scientific law of gravity immediately becomes something to think about—like it or not.

Also, we need to understand the difference between a scientific law and a theory. While a law is something that is observable in every known case, a theory is something that someone **thinks** might have happened in the past or might happen in the future. Over the years, many false theories have had to be thrown out because they did not agree with the scientific laws of nature. If a theory goes against a scientific law of nature, then the theory is not correct and it must be discarded.

THE LAWS OF THERMODYNAMICS

So, what scientific law do we observe when we see things wearing out over time? We are seeing the Second Law of Thermodynamics in action. Even though this law may sound complicated, it really is not difficult to understand. Thermodynamics is just a long word used to discuss the way that matter and energy behave in nature. Stated simply, the Second Law of Thermodynamics says that matter and energy are moving toward a less usable, more disorderly state called "entropy." Isaac Asimov, a famous evolutionist, said this about the Second Law: "Another way of stating the Second Law, then, is: 'The universe is constantly getting more disorderly.'" For instance, when a person puts gasoline into a vehicle, the energy in that gasoline is usable, but after the gasoline burns, much of the energy escapes into the atmosphere and cannot be used again.

That brings us to the First Law of Thermodynamics. The First Law states that no energy can be created or destroyed in nature. The gasoline in the car burns, and much of the energy escapes into the atmosphere and cannot be used again, but it is not destroyed. The First and Second Laws of Thermodynamics have been tested time and again, and they are as universally true as any known scientific law can be.

EVOLUTION IS AGAINST THE LAWS

The two laws of thermodynamics present a serious problem for the theory of evolution, **because the theory of evolution cannot be true** if the laws of thermodynamics are true. Let's see why.

The First Law states that energy can neither be created nor destroyed in nature. If energy cannot be created in nature, how did all the energy get here? Evolution cannot answer that question. However, creation can. Since God is outside of nature, the First Law of Thermodynamics does not apply to Him, and He could create the Universe with all the energy it would ever need.

The Second Law presents an even bigger problem for the theory of evolution. George Gaylord Simpson was one of the most famous evolutionists of his day. Listen to him describe the theory of evolution: "Evolution is a fully natural process...by which all living things, past or present, have since developed, divergently and pro-gressively." He explained that the theory of evolution is supposed to be a process by which things develop **pro-gressively**. According to the theory, things started out very simple, and over a very long period of time, they became increasingly more complex. For instance, a single-celled amoeba supposedly developed into a 100-trillion-celled human over hundreds of millions of years.

But when the theory of evolution is placed beside the Second Law of Thermodynamics, the two do not agree. Things in this Universe do not get progressively better over time; they get progressively worse (entropy). Every year, we humans burn resources that can never be replaced. Cars wear out, bodies get old and wrinkly, and buildings deteriorate. If a huge pile of old scrap wood lays in a grassy yard, will it turn into a new house if left alone for hundreds of years? Of course not! In fact, anyone who has done his or her homework on the Second Law knows that if things continue as they are, at some point in the future (although it may be many thousands of years away) there will be no more usable energy.

This Universe is digressive, not progressive, and that goes directly against the theory of evolution. Creation, on the other hand, falls in line perfectly with the Second Law. In the beginning, God created everything to be very good, but since that time things have deteriorated.

EVOLUTION'S COUNTERATTACK

Wait just a minute! Evolutionists claim that the Second Law does not always apply to our Earth. They claim that the law only applies to "closed" systems that do not receive any outside energy. And since the Sun is constantly bathing our Earth with energy, then it is not a closed system and the law does not apply.

This defense of evolution has two problems. First, it ignores the fact that no one has ever seen a true "closed system" in nature (except perhaps the Universe itself). Every system that we study is in some way being acted upon by energy from other systems, and yet the Second Law still dominates every system that has been observed in the Universe.

Second, when energy is added to a system, it only causes the system to deteriorate more quickly if there is no way to use and control the energy. For instance, suppose you have a huge pile of computer parts on a table and the Sun beats down on it every day. Will the increased energy offered by the Sun help the computer parts to progress into a laptop? No chance. Most likely the hot Sun will melt the parts and add even more entropy. The Sun beats down on this Earth every day, yet in every known case we still observe entropy increasing and things going from a state of order to disorder.

CONCLUSION

When the cold, hard facts are placed on the table, the proven scientific laws of thermodynamics disprove the theory of evolution and verify the idea of Creation. The First Law shows that the Universe must have had a beginning and the Second Law shows that the evolutionary idea of things progressing from simple to complex goes against the evidence. Roger Lewin, another well-known evolutionist, once said: "One problem biologists have faced is the apparent contradiction by evolution of the second law of thermodynamics. Systems should decay through time, giving less, not more, order." Indeed, all concrete observation shows this Universe to be wearing down. Once again we are faced with the fact that the ideas of creation and evolution stand on opposite sides of the battlefield—and the evidence supports only one: creation.

But let us also learn another lesson from these laws of science. Just as things deteriorate in nature, so your faith in God and your spiritual strength will deteriorate if you do not constantly "feed" yourself with the Word of God, prayer, and service to others. Let's challenge ourselves and one another to make progress in our spiritual lives, and not increase in spiritual entropy.

STUDY QUESTIONS

1. What is a scientific law?

2. What is a theory?

3. What should occur if a theory disagrees with a law?

4. What has happened with the theory of evolution, even though it goes against several scientific laws? Why do you think that is the case?

5. In your own words, state the First and Second Laws of Thermodynamics.

6. What is entropy?

7. Do scientists make scientific laws? If not, what is their relationship with them?

8. How do scientific laws make a difference in your life?

9. How do the laws of thermodynamics relate to the creation/evolution controversy?

10. Which law of thermodynamics does Exodus 20:11 discuss?

11. Read Hebrews 1:3 and Colossians 1:17. What is Jesus' relationship with the laws of nature?

12. What will happen someday to nature and its laws (2 Peter 3:10-12)? Are you ready for that to happen? If not, how can you get ready?

13. Why do scientific laws not apply to God?

14. Discuss how the laws of thermodynamics agree perfectly with the Bible.

15. What happens to our spiritual lives if they are neglected? What areas in your life have been neglected?

"Then God said, 'Let the earth bring forth the living creature according to its kind: cattle and creeping thing and beast of the earth, each according to its kind'; and it was so."

Genesis 1:24

Sure, a finch can have a baby with a different beak size, feather color, or body size. But the baby will always be a finch.

FACT

EVOLUTION—
SMALL AND GREAT

An ongoing discussion about creation and evolution took place about three days a week at a lunch table in the Smithville High cafeteria. The two main disputants were Eugene Lepton and Jason Jones. Both of their fathers were biology professors; Eugene's dad taught at the state university in town, and Jason's dad taught at the Christian college about thirty minutes east of town. This particular Friday's lunch period found the two involved in a heated debate.

"People who believe in God and creation are ignorant because they refuse to look at the facts," said Eugene with a mouth full of potato chips.

"And what 'facts' are you talking about?," asked Jason.

"To start with," retorted Eugene "the fact that animals change over time. Just look at the finches on the Galapagos Islands and you can see for yourself. If animals can change a little over a short period of time, then they can change a lot over a long period of time." Jason was stumped. He had heard about the Galapagos finches changing their beak sizes, but he did not know how that fit into the creation/evolution debate. "Well," replied Jason, "I guess...." But before he could finish, the bell for fifth period rang. "Well I guess we will just have to finish this discussion Monday," replied Jason, as he tried to hide his relief. That weekend, Jason read books, searched the Internet, talked to his dad, and telephoned a place called Apologetics Press to try to find answers. Here are some of the things he discovered.

ALL CHANGE IS NOT THE SAME

The word "evolution" can have many different meanings. Basically, the word means, "to unroll, unfold, or change." Anything can "evolve" or change over a period of time. For instance, the body style of the Chevrolet Camaro certainly has "evolved" since the 1960s. However, when most people think of evolution, they do not think about small changes such as the design of a car. In the present day, the word evolution brings to mind thoughts of an amoeba gradually changing over millions of years into a human. So, in order to determine whether or not evolution is true, we must clarify what kind of "change" we are discussing.

Small "Evolution" and Charles Darwin

Charles Darwin did not always believe in evolution. In fact, at one time in his life he believed in God as the Creator. But as he grew older, he changed his view and began to think that natural forces, not God, created this world. One of the reasons for his change in thinking came from a misunderstanding of the Bible. In Darwin's day, the Church of England misunderstood the biblical account of creation. The book of Genesis says that animals reproduce "according to their kind" (Genesis 1:21). That means that an elephant will always give birth to a baby elephant and a finch will always give birth to a baby finch. However, the Church of England confused the biblical word "kind" with the biologists' word "species." The Church of England taught that God had created every different species in the world—an idea that came to be known as "fixity of species." The problem with this view was that it simply was not true; people had misunderstood what the Bible said. When Darwin went on a trip around the world to study animal and plant life, he discovered that species are not fixed, but can (and do) change.

Darwin's Finches

When Charles Darwin visited the Galapagos Islands, he found something that was very interesting. On these islands he found several different species of finches, all of which were unique to the islands (meaning that they did not live anywhere else in the world). The basic difference between these species was the size and shape of their beaks. Some of the finches had short, thick beaks used to crack open seeds, while others had long, thin beaks that could be used to catch insects or drink nectar from flowers. As he studied the birds, he came to the conclusion that the finches were very similar and must have been related. In fact, Darwin believed that the different species had originally come from a single flock of birds that were all one species. He guessed that long before he had arrived on the islands, a storm must have blown this flock of birds to the Galapagos Islands. The birds with long, thin beaks stayed together and ate insects, while the birds with short, stout beaks moved to the places on the islands where they could find seeds. Eventually, each group became its own species. Darwin called this process "natural selection." He had discovered that the old idea of "fixity of species" was incorrect. Species were not "fixed" as the Church of England taught that they were.

Darwin also thought that if nature could change one species of finches into several different species, then it could change an amoeba into a man. But Darwin made a major mistake in his thinking. He did not realize that small changes have limits. For instance, suppose it takes you nine minutes to run one mile. But you decide to exercise and get into shape, and every week for the first three weeks you run the mile one minute faster. Does that mean that you will be running a mile in **zero** minutes by the ninth week of your training? Of course it doesn't. Eventually you will reach a point when you cannot run any faster.

In the same way, the finches could (and did) change in some minor details like the size and shape of their beaks, but they did not change any major details like growing hair instead of feathers, or arms instead of wings. In fact, the finches did not even change into other kinds of birds. If Darwin had properly understood the book of Genesis, he would have known that the Bible does not say that finches cannot change into other species of finches. However, the Bible does say that animals reproduce "according to their kind"—which means that a finch will never change into a mouse. The Galapagos finches had adapted to their environment in some minor details, but they were still just finches.

Another example commonly given as proof of evolution is the English Peppered Moth. Before the industrial revolution in England, most of these moths were a light, speckled-gray color. Their light color blended in with the trees and camouflaged them from birds. A black form of the moth also existed but it was rare because birds could see it easier. However, when the industrial factories in England started producing soot and smoke, the trees began to turn black. In only a few years, the black moths greatly outnumbered the white moths. Evolutionists say that this change in the moth population proves that species can "evolve" different characteristics that allow them to survive.

Once again, however, this "proof" of evolution falls short. For one thing, black moths and light moths had always been around. No new genetic material was created to form a black moth. Also, the moths were still moths. They did not change into lizards or mice. Furthermore, in the past several years, the environment in England has been improved, the trees are turning lighter, and the number of lighter moths has increased. The moths always had the built-in ability to vary in color, but they never had the ability to become anything other than moths.

Small changes like the ones that took place in the finches and moths are recognized and accepted by both creationists and evolutionists. Such changes have been given the name "**micro**evolution," meaning "small change." Microevolution is responsible for much of the diversity that we see in dogs, cats, and other animals. However, even though people over the years have figured out how to breed different dogs to produce the particular species of dog that they want, no one has ever figured out how to breed two dogs and get a cat. Small changes do occur, but eventually those changes come to a point where no more changes are possible.

Big "Evolution"

Both evolutionists and creationists recognize the fact that small changes do take place in plants and animals. However, some people refuse to recognize that these changes have certain limits. They believe that if nature is given enough time, then it will eventually turn a finch into something other than a bird. This idea of "big change" is often called "**macro**evolution" (also known as the "General Theory of Evolution"). This idea basically states that all living things originated from a single life form billions of years ago. And, by a series of changes over millions of years, this life form "evolved" into different creatures such as fish, lizards, monkeys, and man.

The problem with "macroevolution" is that it goes against what we have observed in nature, in that it does not recognize the limits of change. No one has ever seen a finch produce anything other than a finch. Sure, a finch can have a baby with a different beak size, feather color, or body size. But the baby will always be a finch.

CONCLUSION

Charles Darwin did some things right. He looked closely at nature and rejected the incorrect idea of "fixity of species" based on the factual evidence that he found. However, he was wrong to go beyond the facts and refuse to recognize that change has built-in limits. If the Church of England had not misunderstood the Bible, then things might be different today. Let this be a lesson to all of us. We must all study the Bible so we can properly understand it and teach it, and we must be honest with the facts of nature. When both are correctly understood, they will not disagree.

Oh, and by the way, after Jason went back to the lunch table the next Monday armed with this information, Eugene was much less eager to debate the topic any more.

STUDY QUESTIONS

1. What did Charles Darwin do right when looking at the evidence for "fixity of species?" What did he do wrong?

2. Read James 3:17. How does this verse say we should react when we are presented with facts that go against wrong ideas that we hold?

3. What does the word "evolution" actually mean?

4. What do most people in our society mean when they use the word evolution?

5. What two types of evolution were discussed in this chapter? Explain the differences between them.

6. When have you been in a discussion with a teacher or classmate who argued for evolution? What information did they use to argue for evolution? What information did you use to present the idea of creation? Are you prepared for another such discussion? If not, how will you get prepared?

7. Many of you will be studying this book in a Bible class. Why do you think we are discussing Darwin and finches in Bible class and not science class?

8. How did a misunderstanding of the Bible lead Darwin away from the truth? What does that say about the importance of properly understanding the Bible?

9. What instructions do Ephesians 3:4 and 2 Timothy 2:15 give us in regard to understanding the Bible?

"Then God saw everything that He had made, and indeed it was very good."

Genesis 1:31

What can you expect from dating methods that are based entirely on built-in assumptions? Anything is possible!

MEASURING THE
AGE OF THE EARTH

I understand that you don't use words like half-life, radiometric, and daughter element in everyday conversation. In fact, I am quite sure that you are more interested in dating the boy or girl in third period English class than you are in studying the methods used to date the Earth. However, since most science books and school textbooks are selling you a lie by telling you that the Earth is supposed to be almost 5 billion years old (and the Universe has been around longer than that), I think you deserve to hear the truth.

However, before we start this study on dating methods, you have the right to ask a very valid question: "Why does the age of the Earth matter?" The answer is simple. The Bible presents evidence to establish that the Earth is only a few thousand years old. Most scientists suggest that it is billions of years old. If the dating methods these scientists use are valid, then the Bible is wrong and certainly cannot be trusted to show you the way to heaven. However, if the dating methods that give billions of years are invalid, then the Bible remains the inspired Word of God that can be trusted.

EVOLUTION NEEDS MORE TIME

Since the days of Charles Darwin, it has become crystal clear that in order for evolution to have even the remotest chance of occurring, it must be given millions of years. In Darwin's day, many scientists thought that 20 million years would be enough time. But as scientists began to discover the intricate complexity of the Universe, it soon became evident that the time frame must be increased by billions of years (I wonder how many more billions scientist will have to add in the future?). In order to "prove" that these billions of years have occurred, certain dating methods have been invented to calculate the Earth's age. If you have taken Earth Science (which is a standard eighth grade course), then you have studied the different ways that scientists "date" the rocks and other materials of the Earth. The goal of this chapter is to show (without going into technical details) that the dating methods yielding billions of years have some serious flaws in them.

CARBON-14

Probably the most famous method is Carbon-14 dating. However, many people do not understand that Carbon-14 dating (also known as radiocarbon dating) can only be used to date things that once lived (such as plants, animals, and humans). Furthermore, even the inventor of the method, W.F. Libby, acknowledged that it is not an accurate way of dating things past about 20,000 years old. Carbon-14 can never be used to get accurate ages in the millions. In fact, one wonders if it can be used to get accurate dates even in thousands of years. Consider, for instance, the fact that the shells of **living** mollusks, when dated using C-14, rendered an age of 2,300 years.[1] Also, seals that were freshly killed were dated at 1,300 years old.[2] Obviously, Carbon-14 dating cannot accurately render dates for the age of the Earth in billions of years. It also seems to have trouble even with items measured in thousands of years.

RADIOMETRIC DATING

The new heroes for evolutionary dating that are supposed to be able to give ages in the billions are the various radiometric dating methods. Each of these methods is based upon the decay rate of certain elements. In one method, for instance, the element uranium-238 will break down into the element lead over a period of many years. The element that breaks down (in this case, uranium-238) is called the parent element, and the element that is formed (in this case, lead) is called the daughter element. How long is this supposed to take? In the case of uranium and lead, the half-life is supposed to be 4.5 billion years. A half-life is simply the time that it takes half of a sample of the parent element to turn into the daughter element. For instance, if you have 50 ounces of uranium, then in 4.5 billion years you supposedly should have 25 ounces of uranium and 25 ounces of lead. Therefore, if you know the rate of decay for an element, once you measure the amount of the two elements in the rock sample, simple math should give you an age for the rock. However, there are certain things that must be assumed in order for radiometric dating to work. Let's look at those assumptions.

Assumption 1: The Rate of Decay has Always been the Same

The first major assumption built into radiometric dating is the idea that the parent elements have decayed in the past at the exact same rate as they are decaying today. This idea has problems, because no one alive today knows what kind of environment existed in the distant past. We cannot claim to know how fast elements decayed in the past, because we do not have any evidence to prove this idea (which is why it is an assumption). Let's consider how badly this idea could alter the age of the Earth. Suppose you come upon a man who is cutting down trees in a forest. You watch him for an entire hour and he only cuts down 1 tree. Then you count the number of trees he has cut—31 in all. **If you assume** that he has been cutting trees down at the same rate, then you think that he has chopped for 31 hours. However, when you talk to the man, he informs you that, earlier in the day when his ax was sharp and his stomach filled, he was cutting down 5 trees an hour; only in the last hour had he slacked. With this information, you now understand that he worked for only seven hours, not 31. Claiming that the decay rates in the past were the same as they are now is an assumption that cannot be proven and should not be granted to those who want an age for the Earth measured in billions of years.

Assumption 2: Elements have not been Affected by Outside Forces

Another assumption built into the radiometric dating methods is the idea that the elements have not been affected by outside forces. That means that no water has soaked through the sample and "carried away" some of the lead, or that none of the uranium had a chance to escape through pores in the rock. However, this is a huge assumption. How can a person claim that environmental forces have not affected the elements in a rock for a period of billions of years? In 4.5 billion years, could it be slightly possible that water seeped through the sample and added or subtracted some lead or uranium? Furthermore, could there be an "outside chance" that some of the uranium seeped out of pores in the rock (after all, evolutionists delight in "outside chances")? If any rock were really 4.5 billion years old, no one in this world would have a clue what had or had not gone in or out of the rock over that vast amount of time. Once again, the assumption that certain rock samples are "closed systems" simply cannot be granted.

Assumption 3: No Daughter Element Existed at the Beginning

To date rocks using any radiometric dating system, a person must assume that the daughter element in the sample was not there in the beginning. However, that claim cannot be proven. Who is to say that the rock did not start out with 23 grams of lead already in it? The lead could have been in the rock from the beginning (and so could the uranium). To illustrate this point, suppose you go to a swimming pool and find a hose that is pumping water into the pool at a rate of 100 gallons an hour. You discover that the pool has 3,000 gallons of water in it. You calculate that the hose must have been running for 30 hours. However, when you ask the owner of the pool how long she has been running the hose, she tells you that she has been running it for only 1 hour and that most of the water was already in the pool due to a heavy rain the night before. If you assumed that all the water came from the hose, your calculations would be way off—29 hours off to be exact. Assumption three, that no daughter element existed at the beginning, simply cannot be granted.

Another Problem with Radiometric Dating

In addition to the assumptions that are built into radiometric dating, another problem is that the different radiometric methods drastically disagree with one another at times. On occasion, the same sample of rock can be dated by the different methods and the dates can differ by several hundred million years. Some rocks from Hawaii that were known to have formed about two hundred years ago rendered a date of 160 million to 3 billion years when dated by the potassium-argon method.[3] Another time, the same basalt rock in Nigeria was given a date of 95 million years when dated by the potassium-argon method, and 750 million years when dated by the uranium-helium method. But what can you expect from dating methods that are based entirely on built-in assumptions? Anything is possible!

CONCLUSION

If history is any accurate indication, other dating methods soon will be concocted that will give even older ages for the Earth. But each dating method that renders colossal numbers of years will be based on similar, unprovable assumptions. All around you, books, television, radio, and many teachers are telling you that the Earth is billions of years old. This is nothing more than a trick to try and discredit the real history of the Earth found in the Bible. Realizing that these vast ages of billions of years come from dating methods that are based upon incorrect assumptions will give you more confidence in the Bible. There never have been billions of years available for evolution, and there never will be.

REFERENCES

[1] Keith, M.S. and G.M. Anderson (1963), "Radiocarbon Dating: Fictitious Results with Mollusk Shells," *Science*, 141:634, August 16.

[2] Dort, W. (1971), "Mummified Seals of Southern Victoria Land," *Antarctic Journal of the U.S.*, 6:210.

[3] Funkhouser and Naughton (1968), *Journal of Geophysical Research*, page 4601, July 15.

STUDY QUESTIONS

1. In Darwin's day, many scientists believed the Earth to be how many years old?

2. Today, how old do many scientists believe the Earth to be?

3. Why has the number of years increased so dramatically?

4. What do you think will happen to the supposed age of the Earth in the future?

5. Who invented Carbon-14 dating? What did he say its limits were?

6. Give some evidence that shows C-14 is often inaccurate, even when dealing with only a few thousand years.

7. What is a half-life?

8. What is a parent element?

9. What is a daughter element?

10. List the assumptions built into radiometric dating. Are they valid assumptions? What do they do to the dating methods?

11. Discuss some other ways assumptions can get a person in trouble. What are some things we assume about people from how they are dressed? Are these assumptions always right? What should we try to do with assumptions?

12. What conflict does the Bible have with dating methods that give ages for the Earth measured in billions of years?

13. Can the Bible and those dating methods both be valid? What is at stake in this conflict? Why should this discussion of dating methods matter to you?

"Test all things; hold fast what is good."

2 Thessalonians 5:21

You are a human being who has been made in the image of God, exactly like your ancestors Adam and Eve.

ARE THERE MONKEYS IN YOUR FAMILY TREE?

Getting the old photo albums down off the shelf is a pure delight for many people. How funny to thumb through the different periods of our lives when we wore thick glasses that made our eyes look like tiny little beads (before we were old enough to wear contacts), or when we had taken a pair of scissors and decided that our hair needed a little work (and so did our younger brother's and sister's hair). Another fun thing to do is to look at old pictures of your parents when they were children, to see if they looked like you as a child. Many times, mothers and fathers closely resemble their children. Now let's consider some pictures of a few "people" who scientists say belong in each of our family photo albums.

You have probably seen the pictures of our alleged ape-like ancestors. Normally, artists draw these creatures as hairy animals that share both human and ape-like characteristics, carry clubs, and live in caves. Most of us even recognize their names: Neanderthal Man, Cro-Magnon Man, Lucy, Java Man. But what is the truth about the origin of humans? Did we evolve from ape-like ancestors as some would have us believe, or were we made in the image and likeness of God as Genesis 1:26-27 plainly states? You be the judge.

In order to look at the evidence regarding the supposed origins of humans, we first must dig deeply into the ground. Buried under layers of dirt and rocks we find fossilized skeletons—many of which, once they are discovered, are stored in vaults where they are better protected than gold. However, these skeletons do not look anything like the skeletons you see in science classrooms or hung on doors at Halloween. Often the weight of the dirt and rocks on top of them has crushed these skeletons, and they are rarely complete. In most cases, researchers find only small pieces and fragments of bones scattered over large areas (some as large as a football field!). Often these fossilized bone fragments are put together like a jigsaw puzzle with many missing pieces. Sometimes, pieces get put together that really belong to two or three different puzzles. But what about all those pictures you've seen on the covers of magazines—those complete ape-like skulls? Most of those images were pictures of casts that had been constructed using a small number of actual bone fragments and a large amount of imagination. From those casts, researchers try to **imagine what they think** the creature might have looked like (you know the ones —those hairy creatures that frequently are shown living in caves). These ape-like, "cavemen" creatures that were supposed to be the "missing links" between humans and apes are far from it! Look at the evidence:

Neanderthal Man

This is probably one of the most famous "missing links." We are all familiar with pictures of this hairy, ape-like creature that looks like he belongs in a cave. However, after examining the fossil remains, one scientist named Dr. A.J.E. Cave proved that this **was nothing more than an old man who suffered from arthritis!** The "Neanderthal" people were nothing more than modern humans. No missing link here.

Nebraska Man

Researchers constructed this "missing link" from a **single tooth**. Pictures were drawn that depicted this ape-like creature (and his family) gathered around a fire. However, that single tooth was later discovered to be the tooth of an extinct pig—once again proving that scientists do make mistakes, especially when dealing with human origins.

Piltdown Man

Thought to be a genuine missing link for over forty years, it was later discovered that someone had faked this particular "missing link" by combining the skull of a human and the jawbone of an ape! Why would someone do this? Because it is very popular and prestigious in certain circles to claim that you have found the link between humans and ape-like creatures. However, regardless of popularity and prestige, no true missing link has ever been found.

Java Man

This "missing link" was classified as a member of *Homo erectus*, the creatures that supposedly gave rise to *Homo sapiens* (humans). Researchers discovered 4 fossils: two teeth, a skullcap, and a femur (leg bone). The leg bone and teeth were, in fact, human. However, the skullcap was shown to be from a giant gibbon (monkey). No missing link here.

"Lucy"

This is one of the most famous and most complete fossilized skeletons. For many years, scientists believed that this small creature walked uprightly and was one of our ancient ancestors. However, as evidence became available regarding the true position of bones for this small creature, it was obvious that Lucy was nothing more than an ape. Furthermore, human artifacts (like footprints) have been found that evolutionists admit are "older" than Lucy. If humans were walking around before Lucy arrived on the scene, then she couldn't have been their ancestor.

Homo habilis ("handy man")

This creature supposedly evolved from Lucy. But a fairly complete fossil skeleton of *Homo habilis* was discovered which indicates that this creature was simply an ape and was in no way related to man. The small fossil that was discovered is an adult female that stood only about three feet tall—as short as, or shorter than, Lucy. Furthermore, the rest of the skeleton was every bit as primitive, or ape-like, as that of Lucy, who is supposedly two million years older than this adult female *Homo habilis*. If evolution were truly taking place, over a span of 2 million years you could expect to see many physical changes that would make this creature more human-like. Obviously, *Homo habilis* was not the missing link some scientists hoped to find.

Orce Man

A single piece of a skull was found near the village of Orce in Spain. Based on this find, some over-eager scientists reconstructed an entire man. For a while, Orce man was said to represent the oldest human fossil ever discovered in Europe. Later, to the embarrassment of many, the bone was more positively identified as being the skullcap of a young donkey!

Rhodesian Man

This famous skeleton was found in a zinc mine in 1921, and was publicly displayed for years in the British Museum of Natural History. Unfortunately, museum employees who were unfamiliar with human anatomy had reconstructed this "ape-man." Since the hipbones were smashed, the designers fashioned this fossil as being stooped over. It wasn't until many years later, when anatomists examined the skeleton, that it was determined to be the remains of a modern man.

Flipper Man?

Scientists discovered a "collar bone" that some believed belonged to a primitive ape-man. Using some fossilized marine plankton at the site, evolutionists incorrectly dated this new "ape-man" at 5 million years old (that's 2 million years before Lucy!). However, this "collar bone" was eventually shown to be the fossilized rib of a dolphin!

WHAT'S THE DEAL?

So what's going on here? Why is there so much confusion regarding human origins? Many people point out that since apes have a lot of the same genetic material we do (and they do!), they must be our ancestors. And so, each time a skull is dug out of the ground, researchers try to determine exactly where on the evolutionary tree that particular fossil should be placed.

Using evolutionary methods, researchers date the bone fragments they dig up, and then they hire an artist to reconstruct what they believe the creature probably looked like. After that, the creatures are described in scientific journals, where they receive their official names. Often these big scientific names tell us something about where the fossils were found (Neanderthal bones were found in the Neander Valley in Germany) or what the creature may have looked like (*Kenyanthropus platyops* means "flat-faced man from Kenya"). After the material has been dated and named, scientists try to determine where it belongs in their idea of evolution.

As of 1992, approximately 6,000 human-like fossils existed. Some are partial skulls, while others may be only a few teeth. Most of these fossils can be placed into one of two groups: apes or humans. A few fossils do have odd characteristics or show abnormal bone structure. But does that mean we evolved? No. It simply means that we have found a variation in bone structure—a variation that you probably can see in your own classroom at school. Some heads are big, some small. Some noses are pointed, and some are flat. Some jawbones look angled, while some look square. Does that mean some of us still are "evolving"? Or does it mean that there are huge differences among humans? Remember this exercise the next time you see a picture of one of those ape-like creatures. Look at a skeleton (any one will do) and try to draw the person that used to live with that bony framework. What color was its hair? Was it curly or straight? Was it male or female? Did he or she have chubby cheeks, or thin? How big were its nose and its ears? How smart was it? These are hard questions to answer when we are given only bones to examine. Reconstructions that you see in pictures are not based merely on the fossil **evidence**, but also on ideas of what evolutionists **think** these creatures may have looked like. The evidence is clear—man did not evolve over millions of years. However, once we have established that humans did not evolve, we must find the real explanation for their existence. Fortunately, the Bible tells the true story of man's origin.

NOT ADAMOPITHECUS OR EVE HABILIS—JUST ADAM AND EVE

"In the beginning God created the heavens and the earth." This is the first sentence in the Bible. The first two chapters of the book of Genesis tell how God created the Sun, Moon, sky, land, plants, animals, and everything in this Universe in six, 24-hour days.

On the sixth day of creation, God said "Let Us make man in Our image, according to Our likeness" (Genesis 1:26). In order to make man, God formed him from the dust of the ground and breathed into his nostrils the breath of life. His name was Adam. Adam was God's greatest creation on Earth; he could walk, talk, think, make decisions, and do many other things that the animals could not do. But Adam was very lonely because none of the other creatures was a suitable helper for him. For this reason, God caused Adam to fall into a deep sleep. As Adam slept, God took one of his ribs and used it to form a woman whom Adam called Eve. Adam and his wife Eve were the first two people to walk on the Earth. They did not evolve from ape-like creatures over a long period of time. God created them on the sixth day of the first week.

Even Jesus spoke about Adam and Eve when He said, "from the beginning of the creation, God made them male and female." If evolution were true, the Universe would have existed billions of years before humans ever existed. That would mean that Jesus did not tell the truth. We know that humans have been on the Earth "from the beginning of creation"—the sixth day of the very first week of Creation to be exact.

CONCLUSION

You are a human being who has been made in the image of God, exactly like your ancestors Adam and Eve. If you had a photo album full of pictures of every one of your ancestors, you might enjoy looking at the great differences between them, but they would all be just as human as you.

STUDY QUESTIONS

1. Which supposed ancestor was constructed from a single tooth?

2. Which one was simply an old man with arthritis?

3. Which one was faked by combining an ape jawbone with a human skull?

4. Just for fun, look around your Bible class or your class at school and note the differences in appearance between your classmates. Who has the longest arms? The shortest? The biggest head? The smallest? What are some characteristics you **cannot** know about people by looking at their bone structure?

5. Before reading this chapter, had you heard about many of the supposed ancestors of man like Lucy and Neanderthal man? What was your opinion of them before reading the chapter? What is your opinion of them now?

6. What will you do the next time one of your science teachers presents man's alleged evolution as a fact?

7. How does 1 Thessalonians 5:21 apply to scientific information?

8. What do the examples in this chapter tell you about some of the information that is presented to you as "scientific"?

9. What should be your attitude toward all scientific and religious information?

10. Even though humans might look somewhat like monkeys, there are some very important differences. Discuss these differences. Also be sure to include Genesis 1:26-27 as a main theme in your discussion.

11. What does it mean to be created in God's image?

"Who is a liar but he who denies that Jesus is the Christ?"

1 John 2:22

Once a person understands Who Jesus claimed to be, then that person is forced to make a choice about Jesus.

JESUS IS LORD

"He's crazy," said many of the people who sat in their recliners watching the 10:00 o'clock news. "He is the lamb in the Book of Revelation, sent to open the seven seals," said many of his followers who found themselves trapped inside a small compound in Waco, Texas, in February of 1993. Heavily armed with automatic weapons, David Koresh and his faithful band of Branch Davidians preached that Koresh was the Messiah sent to unlock the events that would end the world. The United States Government suspected illegal activities in the compound and surrounded the small band of "believers" for 51 days. On April 19, 1993, fires broke out all over the compound; David Koresh and about 75 other Branch Davidians died that day.

Literally hundreds of people have claimed to be the "Savior," "Messiah," or the "Christ." Many of them (like David Koresh) have gathered followers who believed their claims and were willing to remain loyal to their leaders to the point of death. One such leader comes to the mind of any person who has read the Bible—Jesus of Nazareth. Jesus stands as the most famous Savior of all history. But fame has nothing to do with determining whether or not Jesus is the true Messiah. In fact, some people today claim that Jesus was no more of a Messiah than David Koresh. It can be proved from historical evidence that Jesus was an actual person who lived on the Earth, but many "scholars" today claim that He was **only** a person —not the Savior, Messiah, or Son of God. If this is the case, then all of those who believe in Jesus as the Christ are sadly ignorant of the truth. But if Jesus is the true Savior, then those who have denied His deity are in for a rude awakening.

JESUS—A MAN FROM NAZARETH

Throughout its pages, the Bible presents Jesus of Nazareth as a man in the flesh. On many occasions, the inspired writers point out that He lived on this Earth in a physical body like every other man. When Jesus visited the Samaritan woman at the well, the Bible mentions the fact that Jesus was weary from His journey (John 4:6). His physical body was tired just like yours would be after basketball practice or running laps around the track (after all, He once was a teenager, too). Several chapters later in the book of John, you probably remember the shortest verse in the English Bible, "Jesus wept" (John 11:35). This verse showed that Jesus mourned at the death of His good friend Lazarus. Each one of us has lost loved ones and felt sadness like Jesus felt. In order to further prove that Jesus was an actual man in the flesh, the apostle Paul wrote: "For there is one God and one Mediator between God and men, the Man Christ Jesus" (1 Timothy 2:5). Jesus was a man.

JESUS—THE GOD FROM HEAVEN

Even though the Bible writers portrayed Jesus as a man, that was not their total picture of Him. In fact, the Bible presents Jesus as the only being ever to walk the Earth Who was both God and man at the same time.

In the Bible, the name "Jehovah" was used to refer to God, but on some occasions that name refers to Christ as well. For example, Isaiah prophesied concerning the mission of John the Baptizer: "The voice of one crying in the wilderness: Prepare the way of the Lord (Jehovah); make straight in the desert a highway for our God" (Isaiah 40:3). John was sent to prepare the way for Jesus Christ (John 1:29-34). But Isaiah said that John would prepare the way of **Jehovah**. Clearly, Jesus and Jehovah are the same. In addition, Jesus is plainly called "God" a number of times within the New Testament. In John 1:1, the Bible says that "the Word was God," and a few verses later John explains that "the Word became flesh and dwelt among us" (1:14). And in John 20:28, Thomas, seeing the resurrected Lord and touching the nail holes in His hand, proclaimed: "My Lord and my God!"

CHOICES REGARDING JESUS OF NAZARETH

When Jesus was put on trial, the Jewish high priest asked: "Are you the Christ, the Son of the Blessed?" To that question Christ replied, "I am" (Mark 14:62). Once a person understands Who Jesus claimed to be, then that person is forced to make a choice about Jesus. There are only three options as to what a person can believe about Jesus: (1) He was a liar and con artist; (2) He was a madman; or (3) He was exactly Who He said He was — the Son of God. You cannot logically accept Jesus as a great moral teacher and then claim that he was not God. Anyone who was merely a man and said the things Jesus said cannot be considered a great moral teacher. Jesus was either a liar, a lunatic, or the Lord.

Was Christ a Con Man?

Was Christ a liar? An impostor? A "messianic manipulator"? Some believe that Jesus manipulated His life in such a way as to counterfeit the events described in the Old Testament prophecies. This required arranging events to ensure that the predictions of the prophets would be fulfilled. Supposedly, Jesus even planned to fake His own death on the cross, but a Roman soldier unexpectedly pierced His side with a spear. Instead of recovering, Jesus died. Then on Saturday night, His body supposedly was moved to a secret place so that His tomb would be empty on the next day, leaving the impression of His resurrection and His deity.

But how could Jesus manipulate events that were beyond His control? How could an imposter plan his betrayal price? How could he know that money would be used to purchase the potter's field (Zechariah 11:13; Matthew 27:7)? And how could a man who was hanging on a cross arrange it so that soldiers would gamble for His clothing? Furthermore, if Christ were just "a really good liar," how could He have possessed the purest and most dignified character known in history? And what sane man would be willing to die for what he knows is a lie?

Was Christ Crazy?

Was Jesus merely a psychotic lunatic who sincerely (but mistakenly) saw himself as God? How could a lunatic answer questions with profound wisdom and authority? Would a raving lunatic teach that we should do unto others as we would have them do unto us? Would a lunatic teach that we should pray for our enemies? Would a lunatic teach that we should "turn the other cheek," and then set an example of exactly how to do that—even unto death? Would a lunatic present an ethical code like the one found within the text of the Sermon on the Mount? I think not!

Was Christ God?

If Jesus was not a liar or a lunatic, then the question that Jesus asked the Pharisees still remains: "What do you think about the Christ? Whose Son is He?" Was Jesus, in fact, exactly Who He claimed to be? Was He God in the flesh? The evidence confirms that He was.

Christ Fulfilled Many Old Testament Prophecies

The inspired writers of the Old Testament wrote over 300 prophecies dealing with the coming Messiah. From Genesis through Malachi, the history of Jesus is foretold in minute detail. Bible critics who wish to disprove Christ's deity must refute these fulfilled prophecies. But refuting them is an impossible task. Could Christ have fulfilled 300+ prophetic utterances **by chance**? In a book titled *Science Speaks*, Peter W. Stoner and Robert C. Newman have shown the absurdity of such an idea. They selected only eight specific prophecies and then calculated the probability of one man fulfilling each of them by chance.

Their conclusion was that 1 man in 10^{17} (100,000,000, 000,000,000) could do it (and that is only eight of the 300!). The idea that a single man could fulfill **all** of the prophecies by chance is ridiculous.

Christ Performed Real Miracles

Christ also backed up His claims by working miracles. Throughout history, God had given other people the power to perform miracles. But while their miracles confirmed they were **servants** of God, Jesus' miracles were intended to prove that He **is** God (John 20:30-31).

When Peter preached to the people who had put Jesus to death, he reminded them that Christ's identity had been proved "by miracles, wonders, and signs which God did through Him in your midst, as you yourselves also know" (Acts 2:22). The key phrase here is "as you yourselves also know." The Jews had witnessed Christ's miracles occurring among them while He was on the Earth. And, unlike the fake miracles performed by today's "spiritualists," the miracles of Jesus truly defied natural explanations. In the presence of many witnesses, Jesus gave sight to the blind, healed lepers, fed thousands from a handful of food, made the lame to walk, calmed turbulent seas, and raised the dead! Time after time, the enemies of Jesus were brought face-to-face with the truth that no one could do what Jesus did unless God was with Him (John 3:2; John 9).

Up from the Grave He Arose

The most impressive miracle involving Jesus was His resurrection. In agreement with Old Testament prophecy, and just as He had promised, Christ rose from the tomb three days after His brutal crucifixion.

Many different types of people witnessed that Christ had been raised from the dead: the women who came early in the morning to anoint Him with spices; eleven apostles; and more than 500 other witnesses (1 Corinthians 15:4-8). When they saw the living, breathing Jesus—days after His death—they had concrete proof that He was Who He claimed to be all along! Luke wrote that Christ "presented Himself alive after His suffering by many infallible proofs, being seen by them during forty days" (Acts 1:3).

Thousands of people every year go to the graves of the founders of the Buddhist and Muslim religions to pay homage. Yet Christians do not pay homage at the grave of Christ for the simple fact that **the tomb is empty—** He lives!

CONCLUSION

Who is Jesus of Nazareth? He had no formal education and possessed no material wealth. Yet, through His teachings He turned the world upside down (Acts 17:6). Clearly, as the evidence documents, He was, and is, both the Son of Man and the Son of God. He lived, and died, to redeem (buy back) those who would believe and obey Him. After looking at the evidence, each of us should follow Thomas' example and recognize Jesus as "our Lord and our God." How can we do that today? We can recognize Jesus as "our Lord and our God" by obedience to His Word, and by being kind and good to our friends and enemies. We can study the Bible with other students at school, visit elderly people in nursing homes, or pray for the people who don't like you. We can be a Christian example on the basketball court, on the football field, or in home economics class. Understanding that Jesus is the Son of God is more than just a mental idea. It is a way of life.

STUDY QUESTIONS

1. Why would people claim to be the Messiah or the Son of God? Discuss some of those people who have done so in the past.

2. Do you think that others in the future will claim to be God or God's Son (Matthew 24:23, Acts 5:36)?

3. What things separate Jesus from all others who claimed to be the Son of God?

4. From your personal reading of the Bible, list some things that make Jesus different from all other men you have known or studied.

5. What trait about Jesus do you admire the most?

6. Basically, there are only three choices a person has when trying to decide Who Jesus really was. What are those three choices?

7. Which choice about Jesus do you believe? Give evidence to support your answer.

8. Discuss reasons why some people might not want Jesus to be the Son of God.

9. What is the most impressive miracle associated with Christ?

10. Why is that miracle so important to mankind (1 Corinthians 15:17-19)?

11. Upon learning that Jesus is the Son of God, what actions should that knowledge lead us to take? Read Matthew 25:31-46 and use it in your discussion.

12. What specific steps will you personally take in your life to acknowledge that Jesus is God's Son?

"And do not fear those who kill the body but cannot kill the soul. But rather fear Him who is able to destroy both soul and body in hell."

Matthew 10:28

We can see that the Bible plainly describes God as a loving Creator, yet it still tells of an eternal place of punishment. So, how can both statements be true?

LOVE, JUSTICE, AND HELL

Just the word "hell" brings to mind the most vivid and terrifying pictures. Most children learn at an early age about the "bad place" where the devil and wicked people will burn...forever. Because of the horrible nature of hell, many people have a problem believing that a loving God would send anyone there. In fact, the idea of hell has driven some people away from the Bible and the God described in its pages. Here is one of the major arguments against hell, the Bible, and God:

The Bible teaches that God is love.

A loving God would not punish people forever in a place like hell.

Therefore, there must not be a hell, or God must not be a loving God, or the Bible must be wrong.

WHAT DOES THE BIBLE TEACH?

It would be extremely difficult for a person to read the Bible and miss the fact that it describes God as a loving and caring Creator. In 1 John 4:7-8, the writer declares that love comes from God and that "God is love." Throughout the Scriptures, God's love for His creatures is repeated time and time again.

On the other hand, it is equally clear that the Bible teaches that there is a very real place of torment called hell. Jesus often talked about such a place. For instance, Matthew 25:41 has Jesus on record as saying: "Then He will also say to those on the left hand, 'Depart from Me, you cursed, into the everlasting fire prepared for the devil and his angels.'" He repeatedly stressed that hell would be a place of **everlasting** torment: "And these will go away into everlasting punishment, but the righteous into eternal life" (Matthew 25:46).

We can see that the Bible plainly describes God as a loving Creator, yet it still tells of an eternal place of punishment. So, how can both statements be true?

The Nature of Love

What does the Bible mean when it says that God is love. In today's society, the concept of love is often misunderstood. Many people today think that a loving person is one who always tries to keep others out of **every** pain or discomfort. Punishment is often looked upon as an "unloving" thing to do. But that is not the case. In fact, a loving person will sometimes cause some pain to others in order to accomplish a greater good. For instance, suppose a mother tells her 4-year-old son to stop putting the hair dryer into his little sister's bath water, but the child continues his mischievous and dangerous activity? That child will most likely be punished. Maybe he will get a swift swat on the leg or have to sit in a corner. The pain or discomfort inflicted on the child is for his own good and the good of his sister. His mother loves her children and wants what is best for them.

We can see, then, that a loving person could inflict some pain upon another person in order to accomplish a greater good. But the problem still remains that **eternal** punishment seems to be too harsh and permanent to come from a loving God. It is at this point that the justice of God must be considered.

What is Justice?

God is not a one-sided Being. He has many different attributes that need to be considered. One of those attributes is love, but another is justice. Psalm 89:14 states that "righteousness and justice" are the foundation of God's throne. What is justice? Justice is the principle that everyone gets what he or she deserves. It is not difficult to recognize justice. Suppose a certain judge in a large U.S. city let every murderer walk away from his courtroom without any punishment. Even though many of the murderers had killed several people out of cold blood, the judge would just wave his hand, pat the murderer on the shoulder, and say something like, "I am feeling very generous and loving today, so you are free to go without any punishment." The judge obviously would not be administering justice, and he should promptly be relieved of his position. In the same way, if God did not provide a way to deal with and punish the sinful actions that we humans commit, then justice could not be the foundation of His throne.

IF YOU DO THE CRIME, YOU MUST DO THE TIME

Another thing that everyone recognizes about justice is the fact that the punishment often lasts longer than the crime. For example, suppose a man walks into a bank with a 9mm pistol, shoots two tellers, and robs the bank. Later, he is arrested, tried, and found guilty. The punishment for such criminal actions almost always lasts longer than the crime. The actual shooting and looting might have taken only three minutes to accomplish, but the criminal will pay for those three minutes with the remainder of his life in prison. Justice frequently demands that punishment lasts longer than the crime. Those who contend that hell will not be eternal say that forever is "too long" to punish someone. But once a person concedes that, according to justice, punishment lasts longer than the crime (and all rational people must concede this point), then it is merely a matter of deciding how long punishment for unforgiven sins should be. And since God is the "righteous judge" Who knows the hearts and minds of all men, it makes sense that He alone should be the One to decide how long punishment shall last.

Furthermore, this "too long" argument goes both ways. I dare say none of us would stand at the gates of heaven and refuse to go in because we think that the rewards are "too great" and will last "too long." The truth of the matter is, the Lord created every human being as an immortal soul. Whatever we do in this life has eternal consequences. When we sin, that sin "sticks" to our soul for eternity, unless we accept God's plan to wash away those sins.

GOD—THE RIGHTEOUS
JUDGE AND RULER

God created this world and the humans who live here; therefore, He knows exactly what should and should not be done in order to ensure that everyone has a fair chance to be with Him in heaven. Abraham once described God as "the Judge of all the earth" (Genesis 18:25). God is the only Being capable of creating, sustaining, and judging the world. The prophet Isaiah said that God's thoughts are "higher than man's thoughts, and His ways are higher than man's ways" (55:9). And the apostle Paul said that the "foolishness of God is wiser than men" (1 Corinthians 1:25).

A first-grader can see the fact that God is "smarter" than men. Has man ever been able to create a living person from a pile of dirt? Can man control the weather or cause the seasons to change? Do humans have the power to make planets orbit the Sun, or control gravity? Of course, the answer to all these questions is "No!" Man cannot do the things that God can do, and man does not know all the things that God knows. Therefore, when a human says that "a loving God would not punish people for eternity," but God's Word says that even though God is love, He will punish the wicked for eternity, who is in a better position to make the call? That is like asking who is in a better position to call a baseball player out at first base—the umpire two feet away from the play, or the fan who is sitting 200 feet up in the bleachers in the "nose-bleed" section who was helping his child tie her shoe during the play. The truth is, once a person recognizes the fact that there is a Creator, he or she must also recognize the fact that the Creator is in total control of His creation.

LOVE AND JUSTICE—TOGETHER AT LAST

Because God is love, He wants to save all mankind from an eternity in hell. But because He is also just, He must make sure that sin receives a proper punishment—like any good judge must do. Therefore He devised a most ingenious plan to accomplish His goal of saving mankind. By sending Jesus to die on the cross for humanity, "He made Him who knew no sin to be sin for us" (2 Corinthians 5:21). The torture and death of Christ allowed God to remain just and yet still save sinful men. Isaiah described this situation many years before Christ even came to the Earth when the prophet said: "He was wounded for our transgressions, He was bruised for our iniquities; the chastisement for our peace was upon Him, and by His stripes we are healed" (Isaiah 53:5).

CONCLUSION

True love always allows people to make their own decisions. And God will not **force** anyone to accept Christ. Those who reject Christ, and do not obey the Gospel, do not have the debt of their sins washed away by His cleansing blood. Therefore, according to the principle of justice, they must pay for their sins with their own souls.

Since God is love, He has given humans every possible chance to repent and be saved from hell. But the truth of the matter is, some people will never be obedient to God no matter how many chances they are given.

In Revelation 16:9, the Bible tells of a group of wicked men who suffered greatly at the hand of God, yet "they did not repent and give Him the glory." It is reported that the secular philosopher Friedrich Nietzsche said, "I would rather be in hell forever than to be with your God." He—along with all the others who reject God's plan of salvation—has made his choice.

The concept of hell is indeed somewhat "hard to swallow," but it does not contradict the infinite love and justice of the Heavenly Father. The Bible tells us plainly that God will send people to hell forever; make the choice not to be one of them.

[AUTHOR'S NOTE: The basic idea for this chapter came from a taped sermon presented by Wayne Jackson.]

STUDY QUESTIONS

1. In your own words, explain the reason discussed in this chapter why some say that hell cannot be real.

2. What were your thoughts on hell before you studied this chapter? Did you change any of those thoughts? If so, how?

3. Give some places where the Bible talks about hell.

4. Did Jesus talk very much about hell?

5. How does the Bible describe hell?

6. In your opinion, what is the worst characteristic of hell? Why?

7. Explain the biblical concept of love.

8. Explain the biblical concept of justice, using verses like Proverbs 17:15, Proverbs 24:23-25, and Exodus 23:7.

9. How can God be both loving and just at the same time?

10. Discuss some commonly accepted characteristics of punishment.

11. Who is in the best position to decide what type of punishment is appropriate for people? Why? Give some Bible verses to validate your answer.

12. Whose fault is it that people will be in hell?

13. What has God done to keep people out of hell? Use verses like Isaiah 53:5 and Hebrews 10:29-31 to help with your answer.

14. What must you do so that you do not spend eternity in hell?

"And you shall know the truth, and the truth shall make you free."

John 8:32

Adolf Hitler: "Thus there results the subjection of a number of people under the will, often of only a few persons, a subjection based simply upon the right of the stronger, a right which, as we see in Nature, can be regarded as the sole conceivable right, because it is founded on reason."

IDEAS HAVE CONSEQUENCES

Some of you might be thinking to yourselves, "What does it matter if I believe in creation or evolution, the Bible, and God?" You might be thinking that it is "just" a belief, or a bunch of words and arguments that have very little to do with "real life." If you are thinking that, let me politely suggest that you may need to think again. Your beliefs are the main force behind your behavior. If you believe that man is created in the image of God, then you place a very high value on human life. But if you believe that man is just another animal that has climbed its way out of a prehistoric swamp in the distant past, then human life loses its uniqueness and value.

If humans were just "glorified" animals, what would be wrong with getting rid of the ones that are "nuisances"—the unwanted (unborn) children, the retarded, the handicapped, or the elderly? If mankind is just a "naked ape," then "putting him out of his misery" wouldn't be a sin. We shoot horses when they break their legs, don't we?

"No," you may say. "Surely disbelief in God, or belief in the theory of evolution, would not direct anyone into such crimes against humanity."

First, let's look at the principles upon which evolution is based. Take "survival of the fittest," for instance. This principle stands at the foundation of evolution. Basically, it claims that the stronger or "more fit" survive by overpowering or destroying the weak. If we follow this idea to its logical conclusion, it means that stronger humans could destroy weaker humans and be in perfect harmony with the "natural order of things." If you don't believe that anyone would carry the theory of evolution to its logical conclusion, keep reading.

ADOLF HITLER— A MILITANT EVOLUTIONIST

Adolf Hitler claims his rightful place as possibly the most infamous villain of all time. Children of all ages, and the adults who teach them history, shudder at the deeds done by this criminal. His vicious acts of murder and torture claimed the lives of over 6 million Jews and over 4 million other individuals from ethnic groups such as the Poles and gypsies. Gruesome gas chambers, concentration camps, heinous human experiments, heartless starvation, and forced labor are but a few of the images that come to mind upon hearing the name—Adolf Hitler.

One question immediately presents itself to anyone considering Hitler's actions: **Why?** What would allow a man to think that such acts of injustice could ever be justified? The answer, simply put, is the theory of evolution. Hitler believed that the Aryan race was superior to all other races. He believed that this superior Aryan race had the right to exterminate all inferior races since, according to evolution, the "natural order of things" is for the strong to survive. To use the words of Charles Darwin, Hitler viewed his murderous plans as nothing more than "the preservation of favored races in the struggle for life." One writer said this about Hitler:

> A review of the writings of Hitler and contemporary German biologists finds that Darwin's theory and writings had a major influence on Nazi policies.... In the formation of his racial policies, [Hitler] relied heavily upon the Darwinian evolution model, especially the elaborations by Spencer and Haeckel. They culminated in the "final solution," the extermination of approximately six million Jews and four million other people who belonged to what German scientists judged were "inferior races."[1]

There can be no doubt, from any serious study of Hitler's life and actions, that the theory of evolution played a major role in his murderous schemes. But, as might be expected, many evolutionists object to this idea. They claim that it was not the theory of evolution that perverted Hitler, but Hitler who perverted the theory of evolution.

The problem with this line of thinking is that Hitler did not pervert, or even alter, the theory of evolution in order to use it to support his deeds. He followed it to its logical conclusion. According to the theory of evolution, nature has no conscience that distinguishes between what is right and what is wrong. Where would it get such an awareness of morals? Such morals certainly could not evolve from lifeless matter. An amoeba could not evolve into a human who can know the difference between right and wrong. The most evolution could produce would be the idea that "might makes right." When Hitler extermi-nated approximately 10 million innocent men, women, and children, he acted in complete agreement with the theory of evolution, and in complete **dis**agreement with everything humans know to be right and wrong.

Still, many evolutionists will object and say that using Hitler's actions to show the terrible effects of evolution would be like using the Spanish Inquisition, the Crusades, or the Salem witch trials to show the terrible effects of Christianity. The difference, however, lies in the fact that the Crusades, witch trials, and Spanish Inquisition were perversions of Christ's teachings. Christ taught His fol-lowers to turn the other cheek, to pray for their enemies, and to love their neighbors as themselves. It is true that throughout history, people have committed terrible crimes "in the name of Christianity." But it is not true that they were following Christ's principles. In fact, they were perverting Christ's teaching, and twisting that teaching to say things Christ did not say. On the other hand, the deeds done by Hitler in the name of evolution were not a perversion of the theory. Instead, he perfectly understood the principles of evolution, and worked diligently to ap-ply them to their rational end.

ABORTION—A PRODUCT OF EVOLUTION

A huge debate has been occurring since January 22, 1973, when it became legal for a mother to end the life of her child through abortion. Every year in the United States, more than 1 million babies are killed through this process. It is **legal**. But is it **right**? Absolutely not! The Bible repeatedly stresses that it is a sin to "shed innocent blood" (Proverbs 6:17). God Himself recognized unborn babies as human beings. He told the prophet Jeremiah: "Before I formed you in the womb I knew you; before you were born I sanctified you; I ordained you a prophet to the nations" (Jeremiah 1:5). God values the lives of unborn babies, but our society, in contrast to God's commandments, has decided that these precious lives do not deserve to survive.

What could cause a person to look casually upon the deaths of so many innocent children without lifting a finger to stop this modern-day holocaust? The concept of evolution is one reason these murders are seen as justifiable in our society. One evolutionist said it this way: "Among some animal species, then, infant killing appears to be a natural practice. Could it be natural for humans too, a trait inherited from our primate ancestors...?"

When the idea of evolution is taken to its ultimate end, then killing a human baby becomes little more significant than squashing a roach on the kitchen floor. Millions of innocent lives have been sacrificed on the altar of evolution. All who have had a part in these activities will "give an account to Him who is ready to judge the living and the dead" (1 Peter 4:5).

WHAT HAS THE IDEA OF CREATION GIVEN SOCIETY?

On the opposite side of the coin, we need to look at the consequences of believing in creation. If a person believes that God created this amazing Universe, and that He created humans in His image, then human life becomes very important. If a person believes that humans have been created in the image of God, then that person (if he is true to his belief) will not only value human life, but will also seek to protect it. Those who follow the idea of creation to its logical conclusion do not cling to the idea that "the strong survive" or "might makes right." Instead, the principles connected to creation lead people to care for those who are less fortunate and weaker, because of the value of human life. People who strongly believed in creation established most all of the hospitals, orphanages, and civic organizations in the world.

Also, when a person believes in creation, he or she will feel a certain moral responsibility to the Creator. It is because of this "moral responsibility" that many unbelievers have rejected God. A famous atheist named Aldous Huxley once said, "I had motives for not wanting the world to have meaning.... For myself, as no doubt for most of my contemporaries, the philosophy of meaninglessness was essentially an instrument of liberation.... We objected to the morality because it interfered with our sexual freedom." In a world with no Creator, every person can do what he or she feels like doing—without feeling obligated to any moral sense of "right" or "wrong." However, once a person recognizes the Creator, then that person recognizes an obligation to obey his or her Creator. This moral obligation leads people to help their fellow humans, be better citizens, better fathers and mothers, or sons and daughters.

CONCLUSION

What you believe matters a great deal. Your beliefs are the main force behind your actions. A person who believes that human life evolved through random, chance processes over long periods of time will treat life with much less respect than a person who believes that humans were created in the image of a powerful Creator. If a person believes that he evolved from monkeys, then he will act like a monkey. On the other hand, if people believe that they were made in the image of the holy God, then we can expect them to be holy as He is holy. What do you believe about the origin of life? Are you willing to carry that belief to its logical conclusion?

REFERENCES

Bergman, Jerry (1992), "Eugenics and the Development of Nazi Racial Policy," *Perspectives on Science and Christian Faith,* 44:109, June.

STUDY QUESTIONS

1. Why does it matter what a person believes about the origin of the Universe?

2. Discuss some of the beliefs in your life that cause you to do certain things.

3. Are you, personally, always true to your beliefs? Why or why not?

4. Read Matthew 7:15-20 and explain how Jesus said we could know false prophets (or teachings).

5. What are some of the "fruits" of believing in evolution?

6. What are some of the fruits of believing in creation and the Bible?

7. What is wrong with abortion? Use verses like Proverbs 6:17 and Jeremiah 1:5 to formulate your answer.

8. Why do you think abortion is so commonly practiced in the United States?

9. What things can you do to help stop abortion?

10. Sometimes in this life, evil people seem to get away without suffering the consequences of their actions. Use verses like Romans 12:19, Proverbs 15:3, and Numbers 32:23 to explain this situation.

11. Are there some things in your life that you wish God couldn't see? How can you make those things right?

12. Did this chapter change your mind about the importance of teaching the truth about origins?

13. What do you think is the most negative aspect of evolution?

14. What do you think is the most beneficial aspect of teaching creation?

AFTERWORD

Janet wanted out. She just couldn't do it anymore. She had been living a lie for too long, and it was tearing her apart inside. On the outside, to her parents and teachers, everything looked fine. Her grades were still good, she went to church most Sundays when she was at her mom's house, and she seemed to be happy enough. But Janet's friends had started to notice the change. At first it was subtle; she would be a little late to a study group or to cheerleading practice. But as the months went by, she was late more and more, and sometimes she would not show up at all. Her new boyfriend Billy wasn't helping any. He had the reputation of being a "pretty good kid," but not someone a father would pick for his "little girl."

Janet couldn't remember exactly how it all started, but she was sure that she never intended it to go so far. Billy had taken her to a party and talked her into having one drink. "It's just one drink," he had said. And he was right, it was just one drink (she barely drank any of it), and it didn't really affect her too much, except for the fact that it made her feel really guilty. However, the next drink at the next party was much easier to pick up. Within a few months, Janet was an "old hat" at party drinking. In fact, Billy often joked about what a "good" drinker she was. Along with her new-found "talent," she and Billy had started doing some other things together that she knew weren't right. But the drinks numbed her conscience, and Billy really was a sweet guy once you got to know him.

If Janet would have stopped at the sex and drinking, she possibly could have maintained her masquerade for quite some time. But in her heart of hearts, she had never drawn the line at just how far she would really go.

She knew what was being passed around wasn't a cigarette, but when it came her time to take a drag, she did not want to seem like a "chicken." And so for weeks now, she had been wearing strong perfume, coming in late at night, and avoiding eye contact with her mom. The first few lies she told her mom were really tough, but it grew progressively easier to concoct new stories about where she was and what she was doing.

As you can imagine, things in Janet's life started crumbling from the inside out. The guilt she carried was transforming her slowly but surely into the kind of person nobody likes to be around. She was being mean to all the people she loved the most. When she looked in the mirror, she hated what she saw behind her eyes. And on top of all that, Billy had dumped her for a younger cheerleader, and the sight of those two holding hands and kissing after school made her sick. Janet's emotions were a mess, her former purity was gone, and she had learned enough in church to know that her soul was lost as well. She wanted to get out, start over, and be forgiven, but she just did not know where to turn.

The one person she kept thinking about was Jennifer. Jennifer was a girl she had met at church. She was always very nice and seemed to genuinely care what other people had to say. The few times Janet had talked to Jennifer, it seemed like Jennifer truly listened. In fact, several times during the past months, she had invited Janet to youth devotionals. Janet made up her mind that the next time she was invited to a youth devotional, she was going to take Jennifer up on her offer.

The invitation was not long in coming. Every Sunday night after worship during the summer, the youth group got together and had "firesides" where they would eat pizza, play games, sing devotional songs, and have a lesson from the Bible. Jennifer was so excited when Janet agreed to attend. At firesides, Janet was welcomed with open arms. Everyone seemed so nice. These young people impressed Janet. They seemed to be sure of their beliefs and free from the guilt that plagued her. Sure, she saw that many of them had problems, but they seemed to handle them well. A few times at firesides, after the Bible lessons, one or two of the other kids went in front of the group and explained that they had not been acting like Christians and that they needed the prayers of the group. Janet saw what a forgiving attitude the group had, and how much better the kids felt after confessing their sins.

All that summer, Janet rarely missed a devotional. In fact, she even began bringing her mom's Bible and following along with the lessons. She was learning many things about the inspiration of the Bible, heaven and hell, and God's plan to save man from sin by sending Jesus. As she studied about Jesus, she began to admire His personality and teachings. He was not afraid to stand up for the truth, even if it meant dying for it. Also, He loved everybody. He would talk to prostitutes or the Jewish leaders. Janet began to realize that Jesus was the most amazing person in all of history. Janet's life was changing for the better, but deep inside, she still had a load of guilt that had to be dumped. The problem was, she didn't know exactly how to do it.

The next Sunday, she asked Jennifer if they could talk somewhere private. Jennifer was more than willing to help, and they went into one of the empty classrooms at the church building. For the next 30 minutes, Janet poured out her heart, telling Jennifer all about Billy, the drinking, the sex, and the drugs. Jennifer listened patiently as Janet explained that she had been trying to change for the past several months, but her guilt just would not go away. Jennifer gave Janet a big hug, and asked her if she wanted to study the Bible to find the answer to her problem?

They first went to Matthew 11:28-30 and read the words of Jesus: "Come to Me, all you who labor and are heavy laden, and I will give you rest. Take My yoke upon you and learn from Me, for I am gentle and lowly in heart, and you will find rest for your souls. For My yoke is easy and My burden is light." Then they turned to Romans 6:3-6 and read: "Or do you not know that as many of us as were baptized into Christ Jesus were baptized into His death? Therefore we were buried with Him through baptism into death, that just as Christ was raised from the dead by the glory of the Father, even so we also should walk in newness of life. For if we have been united together in the likeness of His death, certainly we also shall be in the likeness of His resurrection, knowing this, that our old man was crucified with Him, that the body of sin might be done away with, that we should no longer be slaves of sin." Jennifer explained that in baptism, the old person of sin is crucified and buried, while the new, forgiven person rises up out of the water with no sins.

They then went to Acts 8:38 and saw how baptism meant that a person's body went all the way under the water (just as the book of Romans had used the word "buried"). Janet followed along in her Bible and was getting more and more excited and nervous. Next, they went to Romans 10:10 and looked at these words: "For with the heart one believes unto righteousness, and with the mouth confession is made unto salvation." Janet realized that she did believe that Jesus was the Son of God, and that she was willing to confess Him as God's Son. She also realized that she needed to repent of her sins, and to be baptized just as Peter had instructed in Acts 2:38.

Jennifer was elated; she went and got Tim, one of the congregation's ministers. He talked with Janet for a while and asked her if she understood the commitment she was making. He explained that becoming a Christian was the first step, and that living a faithful Christian life would take dedication, sacrifice, and obedience to God. He also told her about the joys of eternal life in heaven someday for all faithful Christians. She understood these things, even before Tim explained them to her, and she was ready to make the commitment to Christ.

Jennifer called Janet's mother, who arrived within a few minutes. Many of the other kids had gathered around the front of the building near the baptistry. Janet and Tim waded down into the water. "Do you believe that Jesus is the Christ, the Son of God?," asked Tim. "I do," replied Janet, without a doubt in her mind. "Then," said Tim, "I now baptize you in the name of the Father, the Son, and the Holy Spirit for the forgiveness of your sins." Tim then immersed Janet in the water.

When she came up out of the water, her guilt was gone —along with her sins. The other kids had started singing "God's Family," and they all gathered around her and gave her hugs (even though she was soaking wet). Her mother cried and gave her the biggest hug of all. Janet knew she had taken a huge step in her life, but she also knew—for a fact—that it was the right step to take.

What steps have you taken in God's direction? Are you moving away from God toward a life filled with spiritual pain, like Janet was while she was with Billy? Or are you taking steps to get closer to God by turning away from your sins and obeying God's Word? The decisions you make today will affect your life for eternity. "Remember now your Creator in the days of your youth" (Ecclesiastes 12:1).